Debbie Blank
Luke 21:28

JESUS IS COMING...
SOON

JESUS IS COMING...
SOON

40 Prophecies Proving Christ's Soon Return

DEBBIE BLANK

XULON PRESS

Xulon Press
2301 Lucien Way #415
Maitland, FL 32751
407.339.4217
www.xulonpress.com

Printed in the United States of America.

ISBN-13: 9781545629772

DEDICATION

J esus Christ is my Lord, my Savior, my friend, my inspiration, and my purpose in life. He reached out and touched my life decades ago, for which I am forever grateful, humbled, and joyous.

My family is the center point of my life with my husband, Bob, and our two sons, Bob, Jr. and Dan. God has blessed us these past few years by doubling our family to include two wonderful daughters-in-law, Ashley and Roseann, and two precious grandchildren, Abrielle and Joshua. We love each of you with your amazing giftedness, personalities, and dedication to others.

Our **Living Word Ministries Team**—Tom and Shirley McShane, Dr. James and Rebecca Liu, Art Lindsay, Glen and Ellen Fischer, Sooz Edwards, and Jackie Saylors—have given of themselves through service, support, wisdom, encouragement, and prayer in order to further the teaching of God's word. You are invaluable to God's purposes in this ministry.

Lindy Lazarow, Director of Blue and White Tours, has worked with me from Israel for nearly twenty years in preparing the best experiences for those who wish to visit Israel. Thank you for putting up with all my questions and details for each of our personalized tours and working out the sometimes impossible schedules we design.

Our **special friends, supporters, and volunteers** are too numerous to mention, but you know who you are. You make this ministry happen! It is a blessing to know you and serve the Lord with you while we await His return.

PREFACE

"The sky is falling! The sky is falling!" relates the infamous Chicken Little in the 1840 storybook tale named after him. An acorn has fallen on Chicken Little's head causing him to falsely assume the world is coming to an end. When he sets off on a quest to tell the king, he runs into many others who believe and follow his lead. Over time, his name and statement have become such a common idiom that the Merriam-Webster Dictionary defined Chicken Little in 1895 as "one who warns of or predicts calamity, especially without justification."

Whenever we turn on the news, we often hear a version of "The sky is falling!" Whether it is financial crises, health care, hurricanes, terrorism, scandals, "fake news," or any of a plethora of issues, we are often led to believe that disaster is imminent. Sometimes it is! But, other times we jump to false conclusions based on false teachers or inaccurate information that can lead us to a sense of despair, much like Chicken Little and his friends.

One moral of the Chicken Little story is to get the facts. If we make assumptions or are manipulated with wrong information, we are led astray into fear, despair, and ignorance of God's glorious plans. God wants us to know Him, have hope for the future based on His truth, and then make decisions based on that truth. Throughout this book, you will read the truth and facts and find hope for the future. Then you will be given the opportunity to act on them.

Forty-one percent of our country believe we are living in the time of Christ's return. Therefore, it is imperative that we turn to God and His word to discover what that time looks like. Only God knows the future, and He was kind enough to share it with us in explicit detail. He wants us to know His plans, so we are ready, faithful, and anticipating His return.

This book provides truth, not hysteria, of God's plans and prophesies for the future. It then lays out how these prophecies have already been fulfilled or can be fulfilled at any time, thus proving that we are living in the times approaching Jesus' return. No other generation has seen fulfilled prophecies to this magnitude except those who experienced the first coming of Jesus.

God has a purpose and a plan that will not be thwarted. He has shared that plan with us so that we can be prepared and can have hope in these last days. Would you like to know that truth? Would you like to find hope in what may seem like a hopeless situation? Then reject any Chicken Little hysteria and get the facts through this book, so you can know the truth, because that truth will set you free.

—Debbie Blank

For the essence of prophecy is to give a clear witness for Jesus. (Revelation 19:10, NLT)

www.livingwordministry.org

CHART 1

The Psalm 83 Confederates

Tents of Edom	Palestinians & Southern Jordanians
Ishmaelites	Saudis (*Ishmael father of Arabs*)
Moab	Palestinians & Central Jordanians
Hagarenes	Egyptians – (*Hagar Egypt Matriarch*)
Gebal	Hezbollah & Northern Lebanese
Ammon	Palestinians & Northern Jordanians
Amalek	Arabs of the Sinai Area
Philistia	Hamas of the Gaza Strip
Tyre	Hezbollah & Southern Lebanese
Assyria	Syrians and Northern Iraqi's

CHART 2

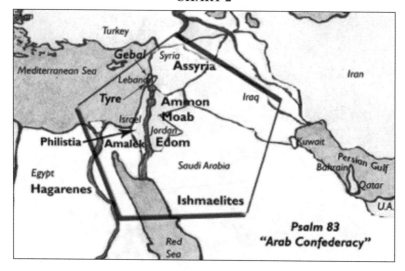

CHART 3

CHART 4

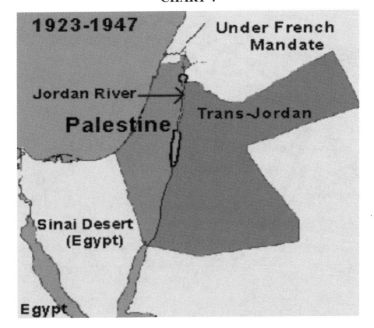

CHART 5

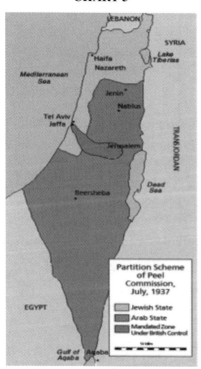

Partition Scheme
of Peel
Commission,
July, 1937

Jewish State
Arab State
Mandated Zone
Under British Control

CHART 6

Partition Plan 1947 (U.N. Resolution 181)

Jewish State
Arab State
International Zone

CHART 7

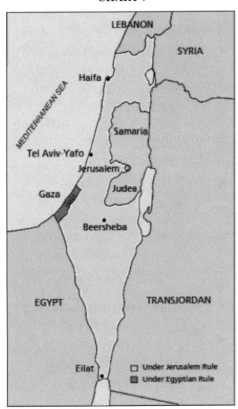

CHART 8

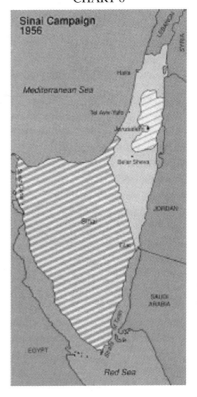

CHART 9

Ceasefire Lines After Six-Day War 1967

CHART 10

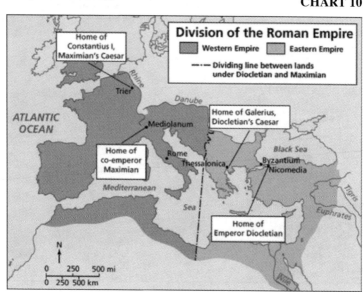

Division of the Roman Empire

CHART 11

Regional Groupings

- Developed regions
- Countries of the Commonwealth of Independent States (CIS)
- Northern Africa
- Sub-Saharan Africa
- South-Eastern Asia
- Oceania
- Eastern Asia
- Southern Asia
- Western Asia
- Latin America & the Caribbean

This report presents data on progress towards the Millennium Development Goals for the world as a whole and for various country groupings. These are classified as 'developing' regions, the transition economies of the Commonwealth of Independent States (CIS) in Asia and Europe, and the 'developed' regions.[1] The developing regions are further broken down into the subregions shown on the map above. These regional groupings are based on United Nations geographical divisions, with some modifications necessary to create, to the extent possible, groups of countries for which a meaningful analysis can be carried out. A complete list of countries included in each region and subregion is available at mdgs.un.org.

[1] Since there is no established convention for the designation of 'developed' and 'developing' countries or areas in the United Nations system, this distinction is made for the purposes of statistical analysis only.

CHART 12

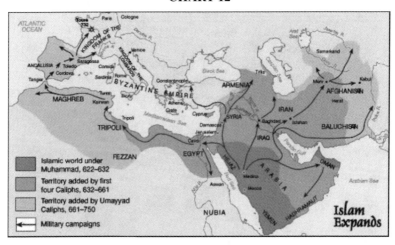

- Islamic world under Muhammad, 622–632
- Territory added by first four Caliphs, 632–661
- Territory added by Umayyad Caliphs, 661–750
- ← Military campaigns

Islam Expands

CONTENTS

INTRODUCTION

I f you are like most people, you will skip this introduction because it is too long or because you want to get to the meat of book. However, if you do, you will miss the very foundation on which this book is established. Because in order to discover the future, you need to understand the past.

What is Bible prophecy? How much of the Bible is prophetic? Why does God give us these prophecies? Who are these prophecies for? Have biblical prophecies been fulfilled in the past? How does God fulfill Bible prophecy? All those questions and so many more can be understood if we go back to the beginning to discover God's actions in the past. Then we can see His plans for the future.

Perhaps once you read the fulfilled prophecies, you will have a hunger to understand the past better. You can do that through this book that outlines the biblical history and foundation for all the prophecies. An even better study would be the Bible itself, written by God for our instruction. I pray you will take the time to know God and His full scope of past and future prophecies, so you can see His character and His plans fulfilled.

Are We Living in the End Times?

Are these times in which we live different from any other? Absolutely! No generation before us could have anticipated the advancements and accomplishments our world enjoys, which have brought about untold opportunities coupled with instability and waywardness away from God and His word.

Just a little over one hundred years ago, most people never traveled outside their towns and knew little of what was happening worldwide. Today we can travel anywhere in the world and even into space. We enjoy instant communications through phones, texting, and the Internet. Our knowledge doubles continually, allowing us to read and discover more than ever before. Even reading one week's worth of newspapers today is more than most people read in their entire lifetimes just a century ago. We have more freedoms and free time to enjoy leisure activities and family time. Due to medical advancements, our life expectancy in the United States has increased from thirty-nine in 1850 to fifty-nine by 1930 to seventy-nine in 2017.

During the Industrial Revolution, the world saw more achievements than humanly thought possible. Who could have imagined cars, airplanes, spacecraft, radio, TV, computers, Internet, and all the other technological advancements introduced in the past several decades?

God created all things good, including mankind with whom He desires to have a relationship. We have thwarted God's intent through our sinful nature. We developed a post-modern view of God as our "Sugar Daddy" or "Santa Claus," just waiting to give us everything we want, rather than as our Sovereign God whom we are to revere and serve. We often see God through tunnel vision, focusing on His love while forgetting His justice and call to repentance and obedience.

The "busyness" of communications, conveniences, entertainment, and activities has shrouded our time with God, thereby putting our interests before God. The corruption, mistrust, disunity, and dependence on our government have so drastically changed our country that nearly half our citizens live off government assistance. Pornography, drugs, crime, persecution, and so much more have destroyed more lives than one can imagine.

The fear of terrorism, nuclear proliferation, unstable governments, economic collapse, world health epidemics, and unstable ecological systems has caused a new global phenomena. We have become interdependent upon one another worldwide in just about all facets of life, thus paving the way for a new world order to place more regulations and restrictions on us. I think you get the idea how these times in which we are living are different from any other time in human history, in ways both good and bad.

These times are also unique in that we are living in one of only two times in human history when Bible prophecies are being fulfilled faster and in more abundance than any other time. No generation, except the generation that saw the coming of Jesus Christ the first time, has seen prophecies fulfilled like we are seeing today. That should wake us up to understand that God is doing something significant in these interesting times. However, instead of turning to God in anticipation of His return, we are responding in just the opposite way.

People are turning away from the God of the Bible to New Age theology, new interpretations of the Bible, cults, other religious beliefs, or no religious belief. In Great Britain, a little more than 1 percent of Christians attend church each week, with about 13,000 churches either closing or being converted to mosques since 1960, as outlined in a Gatestone Institute article by Soeren Kern on January 16, 2012. While 64 percent of the French population identify themselves as Roman Catholic, only 4.5 percent are practicing Catholics, according to a 2009 paper by the French Institute of Public Opinion.

A Barna Survey study in 2009 showed that only 9 percent of adult Americans hold a biblical worldview. Of Americans aged eighteen through twenty-nine, 22 percent claim the "nonreligious" label, a significant increase from 11 percent in 1990, according to *Trinity College's American Nones: Profile of the No Religion Population.*

Along with the decline in our Christian beliefs, our actions prove that we are moving away from God. In 1987, seven out of the eight actions surveyed (adultery, homosexuality, cheating on taxes, pornography, marijuana and alcohol usage, having an abortion, living together before marriage) were considered by the majority of Americans to be morally wrong (alcohol usage was acceptable to 58 percent). Now, only three of the behaviors are thought to be morally wrong by a majority of Americans (adultery, cheating on taxes, and having an abortion), according to a January 2014 poll by CNN.

In the fall of 2015, a US soldier was fired from the military because he turned in an Afghan leader who was using a boy as a sex slave. The news media have reported many instances where journalists, religious leaders, elected officials, and other influential people have been caught in illegal and immoral situations, yet with little or no recourse. When people, who witness atrocities like these, are commanded not to talk about them and see little or no consequences for the perpetrators, that gradually instills an attitude in our culture that abominations are normal and acceptable behavior.

Television, the Internet, video games, and movies open our homes to behaviors that were considered abhorrent and even illegal a few decades ago. They desensitize us to what is right and wrong, blurring truth and righteousness with fantasies, corruption, and immoral and illegal activities.

For those who have strong moral and biblical convictions, our hands are being tied by the "politically correct" police. We can no longer say what we think or believe without fear of losing our jobs, being smeared in the media, enduring a lawsuit, or even being murdered (such as the terrorism attack in San Bernardino, California, in 2015). Businesses and even the Justice Department have forced employees to attend sensitivity training and events to indoctrinate people to their way of thinking. A public school teacher told me recently that she cannot speak about her biblical views or share her conservative thoughts or values in school or even outside school for fear of being fired.

We shouldn't be surprised at all of these corporate, political, and behavioral changes because the Bible said the world would look this way before the return of Jesus Christ:

> But realize this, that in the last days difficult times will come. For men will be lovers of self, lovers of money, boastful, arrogant, revilers, disobedient to parents, ungrateful, unholy, unloving, irreconcilable, malicious gossips, without self-control, brutal, haters of good, treacherous, reckless, conceited, lovers of pleasure rather than lovers of God, holding to a form of godliness, although they have denied its power; avoid such men as these. (2 Timothy 3:1–5)

While many generations could paint themselves with the brush of sinfulness just listed, our world is experiencing a culture that has been systematically falling down this slippery slope like no other time in history. The world looks just like the Bible says it will in the times preceding the return of Christ.

Will Jesus Really Return?

Of the over two hundred Christian denominations that exist, there is at least one thing in which we can all agree: Jesus Christ is coming again. For nearly two millennia, Christians have declared through the Apostle's Creed that Jesus "will come again to judge the living and the dead." The New Testament gospel writers, along with Paul, Peter, and James, all declared that Jesus would come again. Jesus Himself declared three times in Matthew 24:27, 37, 39 how and when He would return. That is why Christians are or should be adhering to the belief that we are to be "looking for the blessed hope and the appearing of the glory of our great God and Savior, Jesus Christ" (Titus 2:13).

Christians believe that Jesus Christ fulfilled and will continue to fulfill the Messianic promises from the Old Testament as outlined in Isaiah 2:2–3, Isaiah 42:1–4, Jeremiah 31:33, Isaiah 53, Isaiah 59:20, Daniel 2:44, Jeremiah 30:8–9, and so many others. The New Testament declares that Jesus Christ will return in passages such as John 14:1–3, Revelation 22:20, Luke 12:40, Matthew 24:29–31, Revelation 19:11–16, and Acts 1:11. A majority of those polled in two surveys believe in the imminent return of Jesus. A Pew Research Center Survey conducted April 21–26, 2010, showed that a large portion of Americans believe Jesus will not only return, but it will be soon. According to the poll, 47 percent of Americans believe that Jesus Christ will definitely (27%) or probably (20%) have returned to earth by the year 2050. Comparatively, only 38 percent say Jesus will probably not (28%) or definitely not (10%) return during this period. Even 20 percent of religiously unaffiliated Americans also see Christ returning during the next few decades. A 2013 Barna Group survey revealed that 41 percent of Americans believe the world is currently living in the end times. But are people living out these beliefs? Are they prepared for Jesus return?

We often grow up with the American values of wanting to live life to its fullest—living the American dream. That generally includes having a job, car, house, TV and computer, family, kids, joining and attending church weekly, and being a good person. We are taught to believe in the basic tenets of our religion, following those traditions with the hope that we are good enough to go to heaven when we die. Oftentimes, we live our lives in that catatonic state of doing good for God rather than knowing and being with God. It is not until we get older and near death that we start wondering who God really is and if we have been good enough to get into heaven. Will Jesus accept us at that time with that attitude? The reality is, Jesus will accept us anytime we turn to Him in genuine repentance and faith.

There are a few problems with that lifestyle, though. First, being a good person and following a religion will not get you to heaven. The gates of hell will be filled with well-intentioned people. Second, we could die unexpectedly, without the time or the heartfelt desire to know Jesus. Finally, why would we decide to surrender to Jesus on our deathbed if we have never felt the need know Him during our lifetime?

Believing in our religion, being a good person, and even anticipating the return of Jesus are not enough. Jesus desires to have a relationship with us. He wants us to "abide in Him, so that when He appears, we may have confidence and not shrink away from Him in shame at His coming" (I John 2:28).

Are We Looking for Jesus' Return?

Think of life this way. If you thought you might have cancer and then found out you did, wouldn't you do something about it? You would undoubtedly see a specialist, do research, explore your options, and decide on treatment. If most of us really believe that Jesus is coming soon, should we not do something about it?

Unfortunately, Jesus warns us that the world will continue to live life on its own terms until He comes:

> For the coming of the Son of Man will be just like the days of Noah. For as in those days before the flood they were eating and drinking, marrying and giving in marriage, until the day that Noah entered the ark, and they did not understand until the flood came and took them all away; so will the coming of the Son of Man be. (Matthew 24:37–39)

While most believe we are living in the last days, actions are speaking louder than words. Second Peter 3:3 reads, "Know this first of all, that in the last days mockers will come with their mocking, following after their own lusts." "The last days" is a reference to the general period of time surrounding the return of Jesus Christ. During this time, the Bible says that people will be making fun of Christ-followers, showing disrespect for those who stand for the truth. We can see that in the life of Kim Davis, a Kentucky clerk who was jailed and sued for refusing to issue marriage licenses to same-sex couples because of her belief in traditional marriage. Eventually, Kentucky changed the wording on their forms, allowing her to follow the law without compromising her beliefs.

The context of 2 Peter, chapter three, goes on to explain that people will be ridiculed for their belief that Jesus is coming, when it says in verse 4, "Where is the promise of His coming? For ever since the fathers fell asleep, all continues just as it was from the beginning of creation." One would expect criticism when sensationalists like Edgar Whisenant publish an erroneous booklet entitled, *88 Reasons Why the Rapture Could Be in 1988.* Radio Broadcaster Harold E. Camping declared the world would end on September 6, 1994, later changing it to May 21, 2011, and finally settling on October 21, 2011, none of which came to fruition. Even when well-meaning, Bible-believing Christians talk about Jesus' soon return, people scoff or belittle them. Their general response is something like, "People have been saying that for two thousand years, and it hasn't happened yet!" Maybe so, but it will occur at some point, and it could be today!

People in every generation have rightly hoped for the return of Jesus Christ. As such, when catastrophic situations occur, they tend to see these circumstances and/or individuals as matching with Bible prophecy. For example, during World War II, many thought Adolph Hitler epitomized the prophetic global leader known as the Antichrist. At the time of the Reformation in the early 16th century, the Laborites and Anabaptists were motivated by such fanatical views of the end times that they led armed rebellion against religious and secular authorities. A Crusade leader of the 13th century, Frederick II, was believed by many to be the one to establish Christ's prophesied kingdom of righteousness (millennial kingdom) on earth.

Attila the Hun and the Germanic Goths of the early 5th century so terrified Christians that they saw them as "Gog and Magog" from the Ezekiel 38 prophecy, thus believing the end of the world was upon them. While those individual occurrences may have looked at the time as fulfillment of prophecies, none accurately matched Bible prophecy. Most importantly, history proves those situations did not deal with end times prophecy because Jesus has not yet returned!

Right before Jesus ascended into heaven, His disciples asked Him if He would be establishing the kingdom then (Acts 1:6). Clearly, they understood the concept of Jesus returning to establish His kingdom, thinking it would occur at that time. So, here we are, nearly two thousand years later, still awaiting Christ's promised return and kingdom. The difference between now and the past two millennia is that we are seeing all the prophecies necessary for the return of Jesus Christ either being fulfilled or having the capability of being fulfilled in our general lifetime.

Does the Bible Prophecy Jesus Return?

Did you know that there are eight times more prophecies in the Bible about the second coming of Jesus Christ than His first coming? That is surprising because it is the initial coming of our much-anticipated Messiah that provided for our redemption through the sacrificial death of Jesus Christ who paid the price for the sins of all mankind. Subsequently, His resurrection opened the gates of heaven and eternity with God for all who would believe in Jesus Christ. Yet, it is the return of Christ that is mentioned more than any other subject in the New Testament except salvation. That certainly shows us how important the return of Christ is and that we should be looking for it.

While we cannot know the day or the hour of His return, we do know that He will return, and we should always be looking toward that day. Titus 2:13 commands us to be, "looking for the blessed hope and the appearing of the glory of our great God and Savior, Christ Jesus." It is our responsibility as Christians to be actively watching for the coming of Jesus Christ. The entirety of the Bible is about 25 percent prophetic. Half of those prophecies have been fulfilled exactly as God said they would be throughout history and with the first coming of Jesus Christ. That means the other half, about 12 1/2 percent of the Bible, are yet to be fulfilled. Most of them deal with Israel's return to their land, wars with enemy nations, and general world conditions surrounding the return of the Jesus Christ. All of the prophecies necessary to be fulfilled before the rapture of the church have already been fulfilled. That means Jesus Christ could return any moment for His church. Other prophecies will be fulfilled prior to and during Jesus' return to establish His kingdom on earth. Those prophecies are the subject of this book.

To Understand the Future, We Must Understand God's Redemption Plan

In order to understand why Jesus will return and the prophecies surrounding that blessed event, we must first grasp God's redemptive plan for mankind all the way back to the beginning.

God created man and woman in His image, had a personal relationship with them, and gave them a perfect environment. Unfortunately, Adam and Eve disobeyed God by eating from the tree of knowledge of good and evil (Genesis 2:16–17; 3:1–7). Death was the consequence, both physical and spiritual (Genesis 3:7–19), for them and for all mankind.

But God, in His ultimate love, mercy, and kindness, chose to give them and their descendants hope through His personal redemption plan. He promised to send a Redeemer who would pay the penalty for sin so that mankind would, once again, have the opportunity to enter into a perfect relationship with God. It is this theme of redemption, which would come through the prophesied Messiah, that is woven throughout all of Scripture from Genesis to Revelation.

After sin entered into the world, God chastised Satan first for his temptation of Adam and Eve, while at the same time declaring His redemption plan that would overcome Satan, sin, and death. God prophesied in Genesis 3:15, "I will put enmity between you and the woman, and between your seed and her seed. He shall bruise you on the head, and you shall bruise him on the heel."

This verse spells out the antagonism that would forever exist between Satan and mankind. That hatred would be perpetrated upon the woman's seed. Physiologically, a woman does not produce a seed; she carries an egg. Who could God be referring to as the seed? We know from Matthew 1:23, that the virgin birth of the Messiah, our Savior, fulfilled this prophecy. Galatians 3:15 further explains that the "seed" which refers to Abraham's offspring, was focusing on the one Seed, Jesus Christ. The passage reads, "Now the promises were spoken to Abraham and to his seed. He does not say, 'And to seeds,' as referring to many, but rather to one, 'And to your seed,' that is, Christ."

Getting back to Genesis 3:15, the passage states that her "seed" will bruise Satan's head (crushing fatal blow) while Satan will bruise his heel (temporary physical harm). Since the seed is Jesus, that means Satan would do everything in his power to try to destroy Jesus, so He could not redeem mankind. But, Satan's attempts would be thwarted by Christ's personal willingness to lay down His life for our sins and take it up again through His resurrection (John 9:17–18). Some have explained that the bruising of the heel is a prophecy regarding Christ's crucifixion, since crucifixion is the only means of death by which the heel is bruised. Ultimately, Christ overruled Satan's plans at Calvary and will permanently destroy Satan when He returns (Revelation 20).

Genesis 3 is the first place in Scripture where the need and the promise for redemption are given. That promise is woven throughout the Torah, through the sacrifices of bulls and goats, the Jewish festivals, and the layout of the temple, which were all designed to personify the Messiah. Four chapters in Isaiah focus on the Suffering Servant of the Messiah where His physical suffering and His redemption plan are prophesied (Isaiah 42, 49, 50, 53). Virtually every book of the Bible opens our eyes to some new truth, typology, understanding, or prophecy regarding the Messiah.

In the New Testament, the gospels and most epistle sermons prove the fulfillment of the Suffering Messiah through His death for our sins and His rising from the dead. When Jesus declared in John 19:20, "It is finished," He was stating unequivocally that He had paid the price in full for the sins of man. He had become the sacrificial lamb, as allegorized in the Old Testament on the Day of Atonement, to satisfy God's wrath over sin. Peter reiterated that in 1 Peter 3:18 which states, "For Christ also died for sins once for all, the just for the unjust, so that He might bring us to God, having been put to death in the flesh, but made alive in the spirit."

Christ's death and resurrection at His first coming paid the price for sin and opened the door for all mankind to have an eternal relationship with Him. When Jesus comes again, He will do so to judge this sinful world and establish His prophesied kingdom of earth where He will reign as King of kings and Lord of lords (Revelation 19:15, 16).

There are dozens of prophecies throughout the Old and New Testaments regarding Christ's reign with His people on earth.

> The King of Israel, the Lord, is in your midst; You will fear disaster no more... Indeed, I will give you renown and praise among all the people of the earth, when I restore your fortunes before your eyes. (Zephaniah 3:15, 20)

> And the Lord will be the king over all the earth. In that day, the Lord will be the only one, and His name the only one. (Zechariah 14:9)

Blessed and holy is the one who has a part in the first resurrection; over these the second death has no power, but they will be priests of God and of Christ and will reign with Him for a thousand years. (Revelation 20:6)

God has shown us in His word the prophecies, proofs, and promises of redemption through Jesus Christ. But, in the ancient world, people couldn't read or write, and the Bible wasn't available to individuals until the invention of the printing press in the 15th century. So, what was God's plan to inform and transform people through the understanding of this redemption plan? He chose a people group, a nation set apart to God, to whom He would give His oracles, covenants, law, promises, and lineage (Romans 3:2; 9:3–4).

To Understand the Future, We Must Meet God's Chosen People

How can we know that Jesus is really the Messiah unless we have something that tells us so? God has given us that source, called the Bible, which contains the words of God that He inspired (2 Timothy 3:16) and was penned by men (2 Peter 1:20, 21). In the Bible we learn about God, His redemption plan, our Redeemer, salvation through Jesus Christ, prophecies relating to Him, and how to live for Him. These oracles were entrusted to a people group known through the centuries as the Hebrews (Genesis 14:13), Israelites (Genesis 32:28), and Jews (2 Kings 25:25). Throughout this book, all of those names will be interspersed to describe this people group.

Early in the book of Genesis, we are introduced to Abram (later renamed Abraham). In Genesis 12, God called Abram to travel from his homeland to the land of Canaan where God made a covenant with him. What is a covenant? The Hebrew word is *beryth* which means an agreement or a compact. Normally the agreement is between two people, such as in a marriage arrangement, which can be broken by one of the parties. However, in God's case, He alone made this covenant for His purposes and glory. It is independent of anyone's actions. Since God's word is true and irrevocable, all His covenants are everlasting (except the Law which was conditional) and cannot be broken by Him or anyone else, regardless of the circumstances.

God's covenants are unconditional, based on His grace, not on man's response. The only exception to that is the Law which was given to show men their transgressions until the Messiah would come (Galatians 3:19). When Jesus Christ the Messiah came, He didn't abolish the law, but He fulfilled it (Matthew 5:17). "For the law was given through Moses; grace and truth were realized through Jesus Christ" (John 1:17).

Returning to the Abrahamic covenant, God promised Abram, "Go forth from your country, and from your relatives and from your father's house, to the land which I will show you; and I will make you a great nation, and I will bless you, and make your name great" (Genesis 12:1–2). Did Abram become a great nation? Yes, He became the father of the Jewish and the Arab nations as well as the patriarch of nationalities through his other sons (Genesis 25:1–4). Was Abram's name blessed? When he died, he had achieved all that one could hope for: a long life, extreme wealth, well respected, many descendants, and a righteous relationship with God.

God continues the covenant promise in Genesis 12:3 by saying, "And I will bless those who bless you, and the one who curses you I will curse." That has been a crucial verse throughout history in reference to how nations and peoples have supported or opposed Abram's covenant descendants, the Jews. History has proven that those nations who have opposed the Jews have been cursed, judged, and destroyed (see Ezekiel 25:3–4 for an example). Individuals and nations who support the Jews have been blessed. This covenant promise remains in effect today, which means we as a country and as individuals should be supporting the people and the nation of Israel.

The most important promise in the Abrahamic covenant is found at the end of Genesis 12:3, "And in you all the families of the earth will be blessed." Later, in Genesis 22:18, God reiterated the promise to Abram, "In your seed all the nations of the earth shall be blessed, because you have obeyed My voice." Who is this seed? God answers that in Galatians 3:16 when He explains, "Now the promises were spoken to Abraham and to his seed. He does not say, 'And to seeds,' as referring to many, but rather to one. 'And to your seed, that is, Christ.'" Jesus Christ is the seed, the promised Messiah, the One who sacrificed Himself for the sins of mankind so that all the families of the earth can be blessed. Abram would be the Father of the lineage by which the Messiah would be born.

The final aspect to the Abrahamic covenant is completed in Genesis 12:7 when God says, "To your descendants I will give this land." The land of Canaan that Abram was promised would later be conquered in part by Abram's Jewish descendants. The full extent of the promised land was outlined in Genesis 15:18: "To your descendants I have given this land, from the river of Egypt as far as the great river, the River Euphrates." While the dynasties of David and Solomon reached close to these river borders, Abram's descendants have not permanently controlled the entire area promised by God. This part of the covenant will be fulfilled when Jesus returns.

Since God's covenants are irrevocable (Romans 11:29), they must be completed exactly as God stated. To date, the land portion of the covenant has not been permanently fulfilled exactly as God established, which means God must bring it to pass sometime in the future. This also means that God is not finished with His covenant people, the Jews. He will fulfill this promise to them and all the other Old and New Testament prophecies that are yet unfulfilled.

The question becomes, through which of Abraham's descendants would this Abrahamic covenant pass? After all, Abraham fathered several sons: Ishmael (Genesis 16—Arab descendants); Isaac (Genesis 21—Jewish descendants) and six others (Genesis

25—more Arab descendants). God made it clear in Genesis 17:19, 21 that the covenant lineage would descend through the covenant son and his descendants after him—Isaac.

> But God said, "No, but Sarah your wife will bear you a son, and you shall call his name Isaac; and I will establish My covenant with him for an everlasting covenant for his descendants after him... But My covenant I will establish with Isaac, whom Sarah will bear to you at this season next year."

Later in Genesis 26:3–4 God reiterates to Isaac almost the exact covenant wording He gave to Abram:

> Sojourn in this land and I will be with you and bless you, for to you and to your descendants I will give all these lands, and I will establish the oath with which I swore to your father Abraham. I will multiply your descendants as the stars of heaven, and will give your descendants all these lands; and by your descendants all the nations of the earth shall be blessed.

God continued His covenant promise through the lineage of Isaac's son Jacob in Genesis 28:13–14 when He said, "I am the Lord, the God of your father Abraham and the God of Isaac; the land on which you lie, I will give it to you and to your descendants. Your descendants will also be like the dust of the earth... in you and in your descendants shall all the families of the earth be blessed." Genesis 36:12 confirms, "And I will give the land to your descendants after you." God then names this people group through Jacob in Genesis 35:9–12, "Then God appeared to Jacob... you shall no longer be called Jacob, but Israel shall be your name. Thus He called him Israel." One of Jacob's twelve sons was named Judah. It was through

Judah's kingly lineage that the Messiah would come, according to Genesis 49:10.

But this covenant genealogy doesn't stop there! Almost 1,000 years later, God prophesied to King David of Israel in 2 Samuel 7:16 that, "Your house and your kingdom shall endure before Me forever; your throne shall be established forever." Does that mean David has sat on the throne in Israel ever since it was given to him about 1000 BC? No, David died. God was giving David a covenant promise that the Messiah would come through David's lineage. According to their genealogy, that Messiah is Jesus Christ.

The New Testament confirms all of these promises in Matthew 1:1–3:

> The record of the genealogy of Jesus the Messiah, (Yeshua Hamashiach, the Anointed One, the One who would save us from our sins.) He is called the son of David, the son of Abraham: Abraham was the father of Isaac, Isaac the father of Jacob, and Jacob the father of Judah and his brothers, Judah was the father of Perez and Zerah (and so forth).

That seemingly boring genealogy isn't so boring when we realize it proves Jesus Christ's lineage all the way back to the promises God gave to Abram.

How easy do you think it would have been for someone to manipulate all this lineage to bring about a fake Messiah? Impossible! Even if one or two people met the genealogical specifications, they would then have to fulfill dozens of other prophecies of the Messiah perfectly in order to be the Messiah. No one did except Jesus Christ.

When Jesus Christ met all the biblical and prophetic criteria as the Messiah, did the Jewish people believe in and accept Him? No! John 1:11–12 declares that, "He came to His own, and those who were His own did not receive Him. But as many as received Him, to them He gave the right to become children of God, even to those who believe in His name." Why didn't they receive Him? They were looking for a reigning Messiah, a man who would conquer the Romans and establish himself as King over the people and land. They did not comprehend the redemption prophecies that were fulfilled through the Suffering Messiah.

The Jews were looking at only part of the Messianic prophecies, prophecies which are still future, which will be fulfilled when Jesus Christ returns and establishes His promised kingdom on earth. They were looking for someone to save them from their troubles. Isn't that what we do sometimes? We look for or only turn to Jesus when we want Him to save us from our problems or fears? We are not willing to build a relationship with Him because He might want us to do something we don't want to do. Most Jews missed their Messiah the first time because they didn't understand His plan for redemption. Will we miss His second coming because we are so full of our own desires that we are ignorant about Jesus, His word, and His prophecies?

When most of the Jews rejected their Messiah, did Jesus reject them, cut them off from the covenants, and tell them they were no longer His chosen people? No! God made everlasting covenants with the Jews that He cannot and will not break. After all, "God is not a man, that He should lie, nor a son of man, that He should repent; has He said, and will He not do it? Or has He spoken, and will He not make it good?" (Numbers 23:19.) Paul confirms twenty-five years after Jesus' death in Romans 11:1–2, "I say then, God has not rejected His people, has He? May it never be! For I too am an Israelite, a descendant of Abraham, of the tribe of Benjamin. God has not rejected His people whom He foreknew."

God has made dozens of promises, prophecies and covenants with the Jewish people, which have not yet been fulfilled. One of those is the New Covenant from Jeremiah 31, starting in verse 31:

"Behold, days are coming," declares the Lord,
"when I will make a new covenant with the
house of Israel and with the house of Judah,
not like the covenant which I made with their
fathers in the day I took them by the hand to
bring them out of the land of Egypt, My covenant which they broke, although I was a husband to them."

He explains that this unconditional new covenant will be
with the entirety of Israel, but will be different from the law,
which was conditional. He continues in Jeremiah 31:33:

"I will put My law within them and on their
heart I will write it; and I will be their God,
and they shall be My people. They will not
teach again, each man his neighbor and each
man his brother, saying, 'Know the Lord,' for
they will all know Me, from the least of them
to the greatest of them," declares the Lord, "for
I will forgive their iniquity, and their sin I will
remember no more."

At no time in history has this new covenant been fulfilled
with the Jews, so it must be in the future.

Proceeding on in Jeremiah 31:35 we read, "Thus says the
Lord, who gives the sun for light by day and the fixed order of
the moon and the stars for light by night, who stirs up the sea so
that its waves roar; the Lord of hosts is His name. If this fixed
order departs from Me," declares the Lord, "Then the offspring
of Israel also will cease from being a nation before Me forever."
Has it ever happened that the natural order has ceased to be?
No! That means that the people of Israel have not ceased to be
God's chosen people. Jeremiah 31:37 continues, "Thus says the
Lord, if the heavens above can be measured and the founda-
tions of the earth searched out below, then I will also cast off all

the offspring of Israel, for all that they have done." Has anyone ever been able to measure the heavens or earth? No! Then God has not and will not cast off the Jews as His chosen people.

We saw God work directly with the Jews in the Old Testament, but when the fullness of time came, they rejected their Messiah. God, in His mercy and promises (Isaiah 42:6; 49:6), has thus opened the door for the Gentiles to be grafted in to the promises and prophecies of old (Romans 11:19–24). We call this the Church Age. But during this Church Age, God has not given up, done away with or rejected the Jews; He simply has allowed the Gentiles who believe in the Messiah to enjoy the same blessings and promises He gave to the Jews.

There is coming a time, however, when God will bring into motion all that is necessary for the Messiah to return and fulfill those prophecies that were promised to the Jews. At that time, according to Romans 11:26, "all Israel will be saved." Based on the prophecies to the Jews that have been fulfilled in recent decades, we are living in the time period when the Jews will see their Messiah.

God chose the Jewish people to be His covenant people living in His covenant land, to give the world His oracles through their prophets, to promise and fulfill future events, to redeem the world through their prophesied Messiah, and to share His love and glory with the world through them. While they as a people rejected the Messiah, God has not rejected them. Just as His first coming as Redeemer revolved around His covenants with the Jewish nation, so His return as reigning Messiah will fulfill His final covenant prophecies to them. Therefore, the events surrounding Christ's return will involve the Jews and the land of Israel as God woos them to Himself.

For centuries now, students of the Bible have been watching and waiting for the Jews to again control their covenant land, which would be the foundational timeframe for the return of Christ. That prophetic time clock "started" about one hundred years ago, culminating on May 14, 1948, when Israel became a nation in their covenant land.

Since then, we have seen end times prophecies fulfilled or nearing fulfillment right before our eyes—more than any other generation—forty of them to my count! That means we are living in times different from any other period in human history. We are living in the final time period before Jesus returns. As we evaluate all that the Bible promises and compare those promises with everything that is happening in the world today, we see a world that looks exactly like God said it would at the time of Christ's return. That means Jesus could come at any time!

When Will Jesus Return?

As I mentioned earlier, all Christian denominations believe in the second coming of Jesus Christ. The only question is when will He come?

Jesus was very clear that no one knows the exact time in which He will return. He declared in Mark 13:28, "But of that day or hour no one knows... but the Father alone." Again in Matthew 24:42, Jesus stated, "Therefore, be on the alert, for you do not know which day your Lord is coming." He even cautioned ". . . the Son of Man is coming at an hour when you do not think He will" (Matthew 24:44).

However, Jesus also warned us in relation to His return to "discern the signs of the times" (Matthew 16:3). As followers of Jesus Christ, we "are not in darkness, that the day would overtake you like a thief" (1 Thessalonians 5:4). Instead, Jesus calls us to "be on the alert" (Matthew 24:42), "be ready too" (Matthew 24:44) and be "faithful and sensible" (Matthew 24:45) in preparation for these final days. We can only be ready and alert for His coming if we know what the signs of His return are and what they look like.

Let me give you an example of this. The southern United States often experiences hurricanes. Modern technology shows the tropical depression, impending storm, intensity, direction, and category of the growing hurricane. Meteorologists have all the data, so they can predict within a close degree of certainty when and where the hurricane will strike. People are continually informed of it and encouraged to prepare for the outcome. Even so, many people ignore the warnings and have to be rescued or lose their lives.

The return of Jesus Christ as Judge is on the horizon. It has been predicted, is building steam, and ready to approach landfall. The location and outcomes are sure. Details and warnings have been given to the people. Everything is set in place. It's only a matter of time before He comes!

We are living in an age when we can read and discern God's prophecies for His return, and we can prove their fulfillment. While I certainly cannot predict the day or hour Jesus will return, I can say unequivocally that no generation has lived through the signs, the times, or the fulfillment of prophecies like this generation has.

Dr. John Walvoord explains our place in history in his book *Armageddon, Oil and the Middle East Crisis* by saying:

> The world today is like a stage being set for a great drama. The major actors are already in the wings waiting for their moment in history. The main stage props are already in place. The prophetic play is about to begin... All the necessary historical developments have already taken place... Since the stage is set... it must mean that Christ's coming for His own is very near. If there ever was an hour when men should consider their personal relationship to Jesus Christ, it is today. God is saying to this generation: "Prepare for the coming of the Lord."

Conclusion

God is the One and the only One to know, predict, and fulfill the future perfectly and at the right time.

> Remember the former things long past, for I am
> God, and there is no other; I am God, and there
> is no one like Me, declaring the end from the
> beginning, and from ancient times things which
> have not been done, saying, "My purpose will be
> established, and I will accomplish all My good
> pleasure"; calling a bird of prey from the east, the
> man of My purpose from a far country. Truly I
> have spoken; truly I will bring it to pass. I have
> planned it, surely I will do it. (Isaiah 46:9–11)

God has foretold and fulfilled half of the Bible prophecies with 100 percent accuracy. Therefore, we can trust that He will do the same with all future prophecies. He has declared that Jesus Christ will come again, which means that there will be a generation that will see that happen! Could it be our generation? Let me restate that no other generation in the history of mankind has seen the biblical prophecies fulfilled as our generation has, except for those alive when Christ first came to earth. Certainly that indicates that we are living in unusual times, like never before.

Those of us who read the Bible in one hand with the newspaper in the other stand in awe at how God is moving the chess pieces in place at such a rapid pace to prepare for Christ's return. Over the past seventy years, people marveled when they saw even one possible fulfillment of prophecy. Now we see prophetic "birth pangs" occurring with such frequency and in such intensity that we can hardly keep up with them.

I always tell my Bible students, "Don't just listen to what I say, believe what God says: check it out in His word." As you read through these prophecies, research them for yourself in the word of God. Check out the context and cross-references. Then, decide for yourself what you are going to do about it! My responsibility is to be the watchman on the wall, declaring God's prophetic word to you. Your responsibility is to act upon it (Ezekiel 33).

Section One:

PROPHECIES REGARDING ISRAEL

Prophecy 1

THE JEWISH PEOPLE WOULD RETURN TO THEIR ANCESTRAL LAND OF ISRAEL

For I will take you from the nations, gather you from all the lands and bring you into your own land. (Ezekiel 36:24)

Prophesy over these bones and say to them, 'O dry bones, hear the word of the Lord.' So I prophesied as I was commanded; and as I prophesied, there was a noise, and behold, a rattling; and the bones came together, bone to its bone. And I looked, and behold, sinews were on them, and flesh grew and skin covered them; but there was no breath in them... So I prophesied as He commanded me, and the breath came into them, and they came to life and stood on their feet, an exceedingly great army. Then He said to me, "Son of man, these bones are the whole house of Israel; behold, they say, 'Our bones are dried up and our hope has perished. We are completely cut off.' Therefore prophesy and say to them, 'Thus says the Lord God, "Behold, I will open your graves and cause you to come

up out of your graves, My people; and I will
bring you into the land of Israel.'" (Ezekiel
37:6–8, 10–12)

"Dem bones, dem bones, dem dry bones!" Those lyrics
from the well-known spiritual song called "Dem
Bones," were adapted by songwriter James Weldon Johnson
in 1928 from the Ezekiel 37 passage partially quoted above.
"Dem Bones" have done come alive!

Is there one particular event or activity that started the prophetic time clock ticking toward the return of Jesus? Yes! The
return of the Jews to occupy and govern their land after more
than 2,500 years of occupation and dispersion is the foundation
for the fulfillment of scores of other prophecies that we will
identify in this book.

The ingathering of the Jewish people in modern times holds
great promise for Israel and the world, as it heralds the coming
of the Messianic kingdom. Isaiah 54:7–8 reminds us of God's
plans for His people, "'For a mere moment I have forsaken you,
but with great mercies I will gather you. With a little wrath I
hid My face from you for a moment; but with everlasting kindness I will have mercy on you,' says the Lord, your Redeemer."

The Jews are a unique people. They are the only people
who have been violently uprooted from their homeland only to
return to that land to reestablish their national sovereignty. No
other people group has managed to do this even once, yet the
Jews have done it twice!

Three generations after God made a covenant with Abram,
his descendants journeyed to Egypt during a famine and
remained there for 430 years. After their exodus from Egypt
and upon their return to their Promised Land around 1405 BC,
the Jews conquered and controlled the land under the leadership of Joshua (book of Joshua), the elders after him (Judges
2:7), judges (Judges 2:16), and kings (1 Samuel 8:5).

Under the leadership of King David and King Solomon,
Israel achieved spiritual and political success, maintaining the

strongest and largest borders of any time in Jewish history. However, because Solomon's wives turned him toward other gods, so his heart was not wholly devoted to the Lord, God declared judgment which would be the dividing of his kingdom (1 Kings 11:4–12). Solomon's lineage would be called Judah which encompassed the southern tribal lands of Judah and Benjamin with Jerusalem as its capital, while the northern ten tribes would be known as Israel with Samaria as its capital.

Because all twenty of the kings in the northern kingdom of Israel did "evil in the sight of the Lord," God allowed them to be conquered by the Assyrians in 722 BC. Many were taken into exile while those remaining in the land were forced to marry Assyrians. This group became known as the Samaritans.

Eight of the twenty kings who reigned in the southern kingdom of Judah did what was "right in the sight of the Lord," thus bringing periodic revival to their land. However, most of the kings in Judah "did evil in the sight of the Lord." The worst of them was Manasseh. Manasseh seduced the people to do evil more than the nations whom the Lord destroyed, thus bringing God's wrath and calamity on Jerusalem and Judah (2 Kings 21:1–15).

God used the Babylonians to cause great strife, famine, and fear to the people of Judah during three military sieges beginning in 605 BC, leading up to the destruction of Jerusalem and the temple, torture, and death to most of the people and exile of the rest in 586 BC. This was the Jews first exile from their land.

Due to God's great mercy, He promised that He would return the Jews to their land seventy years later (Jeremiah 25:9, 11). This prophecy was fulfilled exactly as God promised when He stirred up the spirit of Persian King Cyrus to allow the Jews to return to their homeland in 536 BC (Ezra 1–2). Nearly 50,000 Jews returned to Israel where they continued to prosper under the jurisdiction of the Persians.

In 331 BC, Alexander the Great, king of Greece, conquered most of the known world including Israel. The Jews lived securely under Grecian rule until Antiochus Epiphanes IV subjugated Jewish practices and desecrated the temple in 175 BC. The Maccabean Revolt resulted in defeating Antiochus, rededicating the temple in 164 BC and providing a semblance of autonomy for the Jews until Roman control over Israel by Pompeii in 63 BC. The Old Testament is mostly silent about the years from 400 BC until the birth of Jesus Christ (except some prophecies) so one must look to extrabiblical sources to understand the history of the late BC period when the Jews were under those authorities.

The New Testament provides proof and general details about the Roman dominance over Israel from the time of Christ's birth until around AD 66. It was after most of the New Testament books were written, except John's five books, that a group of Jewish Zealots organized a revolt against Rome in AD 67. The uprising lasted three years before the Romans finally squelched the rebellion, destroyed the Jewish temple, and much of Jerusalem in AD 70, killed many of the Jews, and exiled the majority as slaves to Rome. Over the past two thousand years, a remnant of Jews have remained in their land with the remainder scattered throughout the world. This was the Jews' second dispersion from their land.

Before the first dispersion ever occurred in 586 BC, God prophesied He would return the Jews to their land, not once but twice. The first would be a return from their brief exile to Babylon; the second would be a return from all the nations of the earth. In Isaiah 11:11–12, God declared:

> Then it will happen on that day that the Lord will *again recover the second time* (emphasis mine) with His hand the remnant of His people, who will remain, from Assyria, Egypt, Pathros, Cush, Elam, Shinar, Hamath, and from the islands of the sea. And He will lift up a standard for the nations and assemble the banished ones of Israel, and will gather the dispersed

of Judah *from the four corners of the earth* (emphasis mine).

No other people group has been exiled twice and returned twice to govern their land except the Jews.

It would take more than 1800 years before the Jews would begin their second return en masse to their homeland. Due to anti-Semitism and persecution of the Jews in the late 1800s, and thanks to the passion and foresight of international Jews, a Zionistic (supports Jewish homeland in Israel) vision erupted, which opened the doors for Jews to return to their homeland.

Moses Hess (1812–1875) was a German Jew who experienced anti-Semitism in such a way that he understood the only hope for the future of the Jews would be an autonomous Jewish country in their original land of Israel, which was then known as Palestine. Leon Pinsker (1821–1891) saw firsthand the Russian pogroms of murder and confiscation of Jewish property, which caused him to write *Auto-Emancipation,* proposing the only solution for the Jews would be a land of their own.

While Nathan Birnbaum coined the term Zionism (a political and spiritual renewal of the Jewish people in their ancestral homeland) in 1886, it was Theodor Herzl (1860–1904) who became known as the father of modern Zionism. As a journalist from Vienna, Herzl witnessed the 1894 anti-Semitic trial in Paris known as the Dreyfus Affair. As he watched Jewish Captain Alfred Dreyfus unfairly convicted of treason in two separate trials in 1894 and 1896, he realized that Jews would never be free from anti-Semitism unless they lived in their own state. As a result, he wrote *Judenstaat* ("The Jewish State") in 1896 that called for the establishment of a Jewish state. Due to public outcry and evidence that had been suppressed during the trials, Captain Dreyfus was exonerated of all charges in 1906 and reinstated as a major in the French army.

Herzl founded the World Zionist Organization and coordinated the First Zionist Congress in Basel, Switzerland in 1897. At this conference, he declared, "In Basel, I founded the Jewish state... Maybe in five years, certainly in fifty, everyone will realize it." Little did he know how prophetic his statement was, for exactly fifty years later the United Nations (UN) approved Resolution 181, paving the way for a Jewish state to be established the next year.

Between the beginning years of Zionism in the late 1800s and Israeli statehood in 1948, over half a million Jews returned to their ancient land. According to the Jewish Virtual Library, the following people groups immigrated during these time periods:

1882–1903 = 35,000 mostly farmers
1904–1914 = 40,000 kibbutz farmers, visionary builders of Tel Aviv
1919–1923 = 40,000 entrepreneurs, industrialists, religious
1924–1929 = 82,000 intellectuals, businessmen, bureaucrats
1929–1939 = 250,000 professionals, speculators, industrialists
1939–1948 = 110,000 evacuees, all professions

Israelis have adopted the Hebrew word *aliyah*, meaning "to ascend," to describe this process of returning to their homeland. It was used in ancient times in reference to Jewish pilgrims ascending to Jerusalem for the three great biblical feasts of Passover, Pentecost, and Tabernacles. While most Jews are ethnic rather than spiritual Jews, many truly believe God is drawing them back to their land. Others are being motivated to return by anti-Semitism, the global economic downturn, and the prospects of better jobs in Israel. Israel is currently averaging nearly 30,000 Jews per year who choose to make aliyah to their ancestral land of Israel.

Is it possible that the Bible even prophesied exactly how the Jews would return in the last days? Isaiah 60:8–9 says they would come home first by sea and then by air, "Who are these who fly like a cloud and like the doves to their lattices? Surely the coastlands will wait for Me; and the ships of Tarshish will come first, to bring your sons from afar, their silver and their gold with them." The phrase "ships of Tarshish" is a reference to the ancient Phoenicians, whose expertly crafted ships were large seaworthy vessels traveling the Mediterranean Sea and beyond. For the first seventy years of the Jewish ingathering, the majority came home by ship to escape pogroms, expulsion by Arab nations, extermination by Adolf Hitler, or anti-Semitism in other countries.

Once Israel declared its independence in 1948, the nation was free to bring back as many Jews as chose to return. The majority of these Jews returned by airplane, just as the prophet Isaiah foresaw when he asked: "Who are these who fly like a cloud, and like the doves to their lattices?" (Isaiah 60:8).

It is critical for us to understand that God is not finished with the Jews, His chosen people. Even though Jesus, the Messiah, came to the Jews, and they rejected Him (John 1:12), He still loves them and has not rejected or replaced them. Twenty-five years after the establishment of the Church at Pentecost, the Jewish apostle Paul wrote, "God has not rejected his people, has He? May it never be! For I too am an Israelite, a descendant of Abraham, of the tribe of Benjamin" (Romans 11:1).

God promised the Jewish nation perpetual possession of a land potentially larger than they have ever known (Genesis 15:18–21). He spoke dozens of times of His reign with them in the land of their forefathers (Isaiah 60–66; Micah 7:11–20; Zechariah 14:16–21). He will return to the Mount of Olives in Jerusalem (Zechariah 14:4) to defend Judah from her oppressors (Zechariah 12:2–9). He has promised them a New Covenant that they have yet to accept (Jeremiah 31:31–34). God never changes (Malachi 3:6), His gifts and callings are irrevocable (Romans 11:29); He does not lie, and what He says, He will do (Numbers 23:19). Therefore, we can depend on God to fulfill all the prophecies to His Jewish people exactly as He said He would.

Several places in Scripture, God promised to return Israel to their land after their dispersion among the nations. Ezekiel 36:24 promised:

For I will take you from the nations, gather you from all the lands and bring you into your own land. Two chapters later, in Ezekiel 38:8, the prophet stated, "After many days you will be summoned; in the latter years you will come into the land that is restored from the sword, whose inhabitants have been gathered from many nations to the mountains of Israel which had been a continual waste; but its people were brought out from the nations, and they are living securely, all of them."

Jesus Christ will return to the Mount of Olives in Jerusalem, the same place from which He ascended, to fulfill His kingdom prophecies. He will come in all His glory and reign over His chosen people in His holy city. In order for this to occur, the Jews must return to their land and possess it. Therefore, the foundation piece in the prophetic time clock is the return of the people of Israel to their land, which occurred on May 14, 1948.

Prophecy 2

THE JEWISH PEOPLE WOULD BE REGATHERED IN UNBELIEF TO THEIR HOMELAND FROM THE FOUR CORNERS OF THE EARTH

For I will take you from the nations, gather you from all the lands and bring you into your own land. Then I will sprinkle clean water on you, and you will be clean; I will cleanse you from all your filthiness and from all your idols.... I will put My Spirit within you and cause you to walk in My statutes, and you will be careful to observe My ordinances. You will live in the land that I gave to your forefathers; so you will be My people, and I will be your God. (Ezekiel 36:24, 25, 27, 28)

As we discussed in the previous prophesy from Isaiah 11, Israel is the only nation to have ever returned to and possessed their homeland—twice. The first restoration brought them back from Babylon in 538 BC. The second return brought them from the four corners of the earth (Isaiah 11:12), beginning in the late 19th century.

Over 6 million Jews from more than 100 nations have immigrated to the land of Israel in the last century in literal fulfillment of God's promises. Isaiah 43:5–6 prophesied this would occur: "Fear not, for I am with you; I will bring your descendants from the east, and gather you from the west; I will say to the north, 'Give them up!' And to the south, 'Do not keep them back!' Bring My sons from afar, and My daughters from the ends of the earth."

It has taken seventy years for the worldwide Jewish population to reach nearly 15 million, after the slaughter of six million Jews during the Holocaust. There were over 700,000 Jews in Israel when it became a nation in 1948. As of 2017, Israel now comprises the largest Jewish population of any country with 6.5 million Jews. The United States follows with a population of 5.7 million Jews. France ranks third with 475,000 Jews. After that, the number of Jews per country drops off significantly (ynetnews.com).

What has driven most Jews back to the country of their roots is a heart of Zionism, the need for a national homeland precipitated by extreme persecution and anti-Semitism, rather than a religious fervor. God prophesied that very thing in Ezekiel 36. He said the Jews would first return to Israel from all the nations and then later experience a spiritual awakening.

The Jewish bond in Israel is more from ethnicity than religion, with 78 percent of Jews identifying themselves as secular or traditional. The most religious (13%) and Ultra-Orthodox (9 percent) round out the lower percentage, though some people question whether these religious Jews are truly followers of God or whether they are merely following their traditions, writings, and customs.

The major religious movements within Judaism are: Reform, Conservative, Orthodox, Hasidic, and Kabbalah (mystic). I was privileged to attend a panel discussion several years ago, sponsored by the Omaha Hadassah Jewish women's organization, which featured the lead rabbis from each of the top four Jewish branches in Omaha. Some of them stated they did not believe in resurrection or the afterlife. All the rabbis except the Hasidic answered that they do not believe in the Jewish Messiah. Their main focus was on traditions and community rather than on having a relationship with God.

The Hasidic rabbi in the panel said that he does believe in the Messiah, and he expects him to come soon. When I asked him why he believes that, he said the world is in such chaos that we need someone to save us before we destroy ourselves. That sent shivers down my spine because it sounded like he was looking more for the Antichrist than for the biblical Messiah. However, religious leaders in Israel, such as Rabbi Chaim Kanievsky, one of the most prominent rabbis in the Haredi movement, have encourage Jews to make aliyah to Israel because they believe the Messiah is coming soon. Perhaps we are seeing the beginnings of the promised spiritual revival among the Jews in Israel.

In Ezekiel 37:12–13, God explained that the Jews would turn to the Lord their God *after* He returned them to their land. The Jews are now in their land, but they have yet to turn to their God en masse. The time is coming when "all Israel will be saved" (Romans 11:26). They will accept Jesus Christ as their Messiah.

Prophecy 3

THE LAND OF ISRAEL WOULD BE DESOLATE PRIOR TO THE RETURN OF THE JEWS TO THEIR LAND

And you, son of man, prophesy to the mountains of Israel and say, 'O mountains of Israel, hear the word of the Lord. Thus says the Lord God, "Because the enemy has spoken against you, 'Aha!' and 'The everlasting heights have become our possession,' therefore prophesy and say, 'Thus says the Lord God, "For good reason they have made you desolate and crushed you from every side, that you would become a possession of the rest of the nations and you have been taken up in the talk and the whispering of the people."'" Therefore, O mountains of Israel, hear the word of the Lord God. Thus says the Lord God to the mountains and to the hills, to the ravines and to the valleys, to the desolate wastes and to the forsaken cities which have become a prey and a derision to the rest of the nations which are round about. (Ezekiel 36:1–4)

When we read the above verses in context with the rest of that chapter, we see a sequence of events taking place that prepares us for the next several prophecies. First, the land of Israel will become desolate, then it will put forth branches and bear fruit. People will be multiplied in the cities, and waste places will be rebuilt with the Jewish people living in their own land. Let's examine recent history to see how these have occurred.

The ancient land of Israel (the name was later changed to Syria Palestinia by Emperor Hadrian in AD 135, which eventuality was shortened to Palestine) was known as a land flowing with milk and honey before and under Jewish governance. However, over the past two millennia, the land has generally been neglected by its conquering countries. The land did experience some revitalization under the Abbasid Caliphate (750–861) and later the Crusaders (1099–1187), but it gradually deteriorated with the cutting down of trees, the infestation of insects from swamplands, the influx of sand via the trade winds, and the general neglect of the land. Due to the poor economic conditions in Palestine under Ottoman Turkish rule from 1517–1917, most people left Palestine, causing the land to fall into complete disarray.

Author Henry Maundrell, writing about the Holy Land in 1697, recounted there is "nothing here but a vast and spacious ruin." Thomas Saw, an English archaeologist, described the land in 1738 as "barrenness and scarcity." In 1785, Constantin-Francois Volney used words like "ruined" and "desolate" to comment on the Holy Land.

Mark Twain visited the land and described it in his book, *Innocents Abroad* (1869), by saying, "For all the lands there are for dismal scenery, I think Palestine must be the prince. The hills are barren, they are dull of color, they are unpicturesque in shape. The valleys are unsightly deserts fringed with a feeble vegetation that has an expression about it being sorrowful and despondent... It is a hopeless, dreary, heartbroken land."

When the Zionists began making aliyah in the late 1800s, the land of Palestine was a desolate wasteland, just as God prophesied it would be in Ezekiel 36. There were few trees for fire or shelter, little vegetation for people or animals, rocks from fallen ruins covered the land, sand blew in from Egypt to cover the shore lands, water was scarce, and rain almost non-existent. Who would want to live in a place like that? Who would want to build a country from such barren wasteland? Only those people who had the vision, passion, and calling to return and restore their land—the Jewish people!

Prophecy 4

THE LAND OF ISRAEL WOULD BECOME FRUITFUL AGAIN

But you, O mountains of Israel, you will put forth your branches and bear your fruit for My people Israel; for they will soon come. For, behold, I am for you, and I will turn to you, and you will be cultivated and sown. I will multiply men on you, all the house of Israel, all of it; and the cities will be inhabited and the waste places will be rebuilt. I will multiply on you man and beast; and they will increase and be fruitful; and I will cause you to be inhabited as you were formerly and will treat you better than at the first. Thus you will know that I am the Lord. Yes, I will cause men—My people Israel—to walk on you and possess you, so that you will become their inheritance and never again bereave them of children. (Ezekiel 36:8–12)

L'*chayim*! To life! When the early Zionists traveled to Palestine almost 150 years ago, the land was a barren wilderness. The Ottoman Empire had controlled the area since 1517, but its local administrative capital in Damascus, Syria, neglected the land, left it underdeveloped and generally isolated from the rest of the world. But Israel was brought back to life, just as God said would happen in these last days in preparation for His return.

The Jewish community in the late 1800s numbered around 25,000 and primarily inhabited four holy cities: Safed, Tiberias, Hebron, and Jerusalem. As newcomers ventured to develop new areas, it took a huge toll on the health and well-being of the people. Early photographs show women sitting on the ground, chipping away month after month at the huge stones, so they could be removed and the land cultivated. The Jezreel Valley was unusable swampland, filled with malaria. The only water resource was the Sea of Galilee in the north. The southern half of the country was desert.

International Jewish organizations solicited funds from all over the world to purchase land on which the newly arrived Jews could establish farms and towns. In 1909, the city of Tel Aviv was created, which is now the cultural, financial, and technological hub of the country, housing over half a million people. The first kibbutz (socialist agricultural community) was also organized in 1909. By 2010, there were 270 kibbutzim in Israel. Their factories account for 9 percent of Israel's industrial output worth $8 billion, with their farms producing 40 percent of its agricultural output, valued at over $1.7 billion.

Jewish farmers used ingenuity and technology from the industrial age to drain swamps, develop an irrigation system, remove rocks, till and farm the barren land, apply crop rotation, import fruit trees, and plant 240 million trees. According to the Arbor Day Foundation, "a mature leafy tree produces as much oxygen in a season as 10 people inhale in a year." Since one typical tree breathes out 250 or more gallons of water per day through its leaves, it is no wonder that the rainfall in Israel has increased 450 percent.

The former malaria-infested swamps have been converted into cultivated land, allowing for the rotation of crops four times a year. Fresh water from the Sea of Galilee has been channeled to make the deserts bloom. Israel has developed desalinization plants, turning seawater into water useable for drinking and growing crops. Israel supplies its own fruits and vegetables and exports them to much of Europe and Asia. They are assisting their Arab neighbors with the same technology, so they can revitalize their barren countries. When we visit today, we marvel at how beautiful and fruitful the land of Israel is. Few people could have envisioned a hundred years ago how God would make this barren land fruitful again with 8.5 million inhabitants. But He has. In so doing, half the Jews in the world have returned to the land of their ancestors. Israel has become the greatest "Start-up Nation" in the world.

Prophecy 5

BIRDS AND ANIMALS WOULD ROAM IN ABUNDANCE IN ISRAEL AFTER NEAR EXTINCTION

As for you, son of man, thus says the Lord God, "Speak to every kind of bird and to every beast of the field, Assemble and come, gather from every side to My sacrifice which I am going to sacrifice for you, as a great sacrifice on the mountains of Israel, that you may eat flesh and drink blood. You will eat the flesh of mighty men and drink the blood of the princes of the earth, as though they were rams, lambs, goats and bulls, all of them fatlings of Bashan." (Ezekiel 39:17–18)

Prior to 1900, the land of Israel was barren, with few trees, foliage, or vegetation. Without those, birds could not nest, and beasts would have no vegetation to eat, leaving the land nearly extinct of birds and animals. Yet, today virtually every kind of bird and beast roam the skies and mountains of Israel, just as the Bible said would happen.

As mentioned before, over 240 million trees have been planted in Israel in the past century, allowing fruit, foliage, and shelter for the birds. Since Israel forms a natural landmass between Asia and Africa, it is the easiest route for birds to migrate between those continents. With the new trees, nearly half a trillion birds migrate through Israel twice a year, with many species remaining in the land. Every type of bird can be seen, including predatory birds like vultures, eagles, crows, ravens, and hawks that God could use in His planned "sacrifice" mentioned above. According to Dr. Reuven Yosef, PhD (in *Wildbird*, Feb. 1995), "During the spring of 1994, staff and volunteers from the International Birding and Research Center in Eilat recorded a total 1,022,084 raptors comprising 29 species" (raptors are a bird of prey).

Elsewhere in Scripture we see a similar "supper" where God will bring the birds to feast on those who fight against Jesus. Revelation 19:17–18 explains that Jesus' judgment on the nations after He returns will include this description:

> Then I saw an angel standing in the sun, and he cried out with a loud voice, saying to all the birds which fly in midheaven, "Come, assemble for the great supper of God, so that you may eat the flesh of kings and the flesh of commanders and the flesh of mighty men and the flesh of horses and of those who sit on them and the flesh of all men, both free men and slaves, and small and great."

Perhaps this great supper will take place during migrating season when half a trillion birds will be in the area. This prophecy could never before be fulfilled, but now can be at any time.

In addition to birds, all kinds of wild and tame animals have returned to Israel. Every animal that in mentioned in the Bible, except for bears, has been seen in Israel. At Gamla Nature Reserve in the Golan Heights, people have seen foxes, deer, coneys, and wolves. It is so much fun to visit Ein Gedi and watch the ibex climb the rocks and feed from the trees. The animals roam free due to the fresh water supply and the caves for them to sleep in. In the same area one can see leopards, hyenas, and caracals. Even a lion was spotted in 1960 by archaeologist Nelson Gluck. There is a safari reserve north of Eilat that is working to bring all the biblical animals back to Israel.

This is the first time in many centuries that Israel has experienced an influx of birds and animals in its country. They have to be in place for the prophecies to be fulfilled. We are seeing it today!

Prophecy 6

JEWISH PEOPLE WOULD PURCHASE MUCH OF THEIR LAND UPON RETURN TO ISRAEL

Behold, I will gather them out of all the lands to which I have driven them in My anger, in My wrath and in great indignation; and I will bring them back to this place and make them dwell in safety... I will rejoice over them to do them good and will faithfully plant them in this land with all My heart and with all My soul... Fields will be bought in this land of which you say, "It is a desolation, without man or beast; it is given into the hand of the Chaldeans." Men will buy fields for money, sign and seal deeds, and call in witnesses in the land of Benjamin, in the environs of Jerusalem, in the cities of Judah, in the cities of the hill country, in the cities of the lowland and in the cities of the Negev; for I will restore their fortunes, declares the Lord. (Jeremiah 32:37, 41, 43, 44)

L ocation, location, location! Most people recognize that real-estate mantra, noting the enormous importance of selecting the right site for a home or business. The phrase was first attributed to a real-estate ad in the *Chicago Tribune* in 1926. But God understood the significance of location long before that!

God declared the land of Canaan to be the perpetual home for the Jewish nation (Genesis 12:7; Numbers 13:2). He put that land into the hands of the Jews through the leadership of Joshua (Joshua 1:2–3). He even chose to put His name on the city of Jerusalem (1 Kings 11:36). While the land was conquered and controlled by others for centuries, God promised to restore the Jews to their original land in the time period before Christ's return.

Yet at the Sixth Zionist Congress in 1903, Theodor Herzl, the father of modern Zionism, was willing to settle for Uganda in east Africa as the home for the Jewish people in order to immediately establish a Jewish state. That motion failed. Uganda was not God's Promised Land, Israel's heritage, or the location for God's prophetic plans. The Jews would have to wait to regain their land.

In the prophecy above, Jeremiah asserted the timing of his prophecy to the time when Israel would regather from all the world the second time and dwell in safety. While some people question Israel's safety right now, I have walked the streets of Israel from Dan to Eilat safely for over twenty years. The point of the prophecy is that during this specific time period, after the land has been desolate, the Jews would purchase fields and sign land deals throughout the entire country. The past century has seen the fulfillment of this prophecy.

Through the help of wealthy Americans like the Rockefellers, as well as international Zionist organizations like the Palestine Jewish Colonization Association, the Palestine Land Development Company, and the Jewish National Fund, Jews have been purchasing land on the open market in Palestine since the 1800s. Land purchases were generally in the coastal plain, the Jezreel Valley, the Jordan Valley, and the Galilee. Some of the land in the less desirable areas, like swampland, desert, or some mountainous regions, was available land that could be settled by anyone willing to do so, much as the US Homestead Act of 1862 provided free land, generally west of the Mississippi River, to those willing to develop it.

As Zionism grew, so did Arab complaints over Jewish acquisition of land. In 1892, the Ottoman government prohibited the sale of land in Palestine to Jews, even if they were Ottoman citizens.

The Jewish National Fund was founded in 1904 for the purpose of buying land directly from Arabs. Today, over 90 percent of the property in Israel is owned by the Israeli government, via the Jewish National Fund and the Israel Lands Administration. When land is purchased in Israel, it must be registered with these authorities and is, essentially, a long-term lease.

After the Ottoman Empire's defeat in World War I, Britain was mandated as the authority in Palestine. They promised, through the Balfour Declaration and subsequent discussions, the creation of a Jewish state in Palestine. In anticipation of statehood, Jews began laying the groundwork for a greater sense of national identity by purchasing more land. However, concerns arose because of the Jewish purchase of land from the Arabs. One such complaint came from Jordan's King Abdullah in a letter written to the high commissioner for Transjordan, Sir Arthur Wauchope, on July 25, 1934. In this letter, King Abdullah acknowledged the fear of Arab leaders over the land purchases when he said, "the fears of the Arab political leaders are supported by the fact that the sale of land continues unrestricted and every day one piece of land after another is torn from the hands of the Arabs." Complaints such as this caused British officials to impose token restrictions on Jewish land purchases to avoid being blamed for Palestinian landlessness.

Professor Kenneth W. Stein proved the early Jewish land purchases in a 1991 paper entitled "One Hundred Years of

Social Change: The Creation of the Palestinian Refugee Problem." Stein noted:

> In the 1920s and 1930s, there were hundreds of examples of Palestinian Arabs voluntarily emigrating away from new or imminent Jewish settlements and enclaves because of economic reasons, Arab sales and Jewish purchases. For example, when the Palestine Land Development Company purchased land for the Jewish National Fund (JNF) in the Acre area and the Jezreel Valley in the 1920s, more than 688 Arab tenants and their families from more than twenty Arab villages comprising more than 250,000 dunams (one dunam equals a quarter acre) vacated their lands after each tenant received financial compensation from Zionist buyers.

Overall, documents show that 52.6 percent of the land purchases in Palestine were in large tracts from non-Palestinian owners, 24.6 percent were secured from Palestinian-Arab owners, and 9.4 percent of land purchases were acquired from peasants. By 1945, the Jews had purchased 350 square miles of land in Israel.

Through the United Nations Resolution 181 of November 29, 1947, Israel was offered and accepted most of the land they now control in their state. Further territory was acquired through wars perpetrated upon them by their Arab neighbors in the War of Independence (1948–1949), the Six-Day War of 1967, and the Yom Kippur War of 1973.

It is certainly not unusual for people to purchase property on which to live. However, only God could provide the specific timetable, circumstances, and detailed description for Israeli land acquisition that has been fulfilled over the past century. God's "location, location, location" is and always has been the land known as Israel.

Prophecy 7

THE STATE OF ISRAEL WOULD BE REBORN IN ONE DAY

Before she travailed, she brought forth; before her pain came, she gave birth to a boy. "Who has heard such a thing? Who has seen such things? Can a land be born in one day? Can a nation be brought forth all at once? As soon as Zion travailed, she also brought forth her sons. Shall I bring to the point of birth and not give delivery?" says the Lord. "Or shall I who gives delivery shut the womb?" says your God. (Isaiah 66:7–9)

The United States pinpoints our Declaration of Independence to July 4, 1776. Many other nations commemorate one specific day as the establishment of their countries. But only Israel was prophesied almost 2700 years ago to be reestablished as a nation in one day, which occurred on May 14, 1948. Happy Birthday to you!

In reading Isaiah's prophecy above, there is a pattern of the nation (she) bringing forth her people before her times of great sorrow. Then, she would later give birth in one day, prior to another time of great pain. The prophet Isaiah also points out that it is only through God that all this is made possible.

With that pattern understood, let's look at the modern history of Israel, prior to and at the time of Israel's statehood. As we have seen in previous prophecies, Israel's modern history began when she "brought forth" the early Zionists in the late 19th century to cultivate the land and develop a social structure in the barren land of Palestine, which was then governed by the Ottoman Turks.

During World War I, the Ottoman Turkish Empire allied with the defeated Central Powers. This resulted in the break-up of the Ottoman Turkish Empire and its territories in the Middle East. It was the desire of the League of Nations to divide the old Ottoman Turkish territories among the many different ethnic groups who inhabited them. In order to help these groups establish new countries, the League of Nations mandated that France and England assist them in establishing a governmental system and national identity. England was commissioned over Palestine, the lands known today as Israel and Jordan.

English, Arab, and Jewish leaders supported the establishment of a national state for the Jewish people in Palestine. In a letter Foreign Secretary Arthur James Balfour wrote to Walter Rothschild on November 2, 1917, he stated, "His Majesty's government view [*sic*] with favour [*sic*] the establishment in Palestine of the national home for a Jewish people, and will use their best endeavours [*sic*] to facilitate the achievement of this object." Later, Chaim Weizmann (first president of Israel in 1948) and Emir Faisal (king of Syria in 1920 and Iraq in 1921–33) signed the Peace Agreement of 1919 which stated, "In the establishment of the Constitution and Administration of Palestine all such measures shall be adopted as will afford the fullest guarantees for carrying into effect the British Government's Declaration of the 2nd of November, 1917 (Balfour Declaration)."

Unfortunately, political entities and lobbying interests persuaded England to give most of the Palestinian land promised to the Jews to Jordan. Over 77 percent of the land pledged to the Jews was deeded to the Hashemite kingdom of Jordan in

1922. The rest of the land promised to the Jewish people continued to shrink under such agreements as the Peel Commission of 1937 and United Nations Resolution 181 in 1947. Each time, while Israel agreed to the terms presented to them, the Arabs did not, causing fighting to ensue among the Jews, Arabs, and British over the future of the land. With no working agreement in sight for an amicable division of Palestine between Arabs and Jews, the United Nations stepped in with their Resolution 181. This final attempt to divide the land into two states would take effect May 15, 1948. Once Resolution 181 was approved on November 29, 1947, Israel accepted the terms of the resolution for statehood. But, the chairman of the Arab Higher Committee said the Arabs would "fight for every inch of their country," and they did, starting the day after the resolution was announced and lasting all the way up to Israeli statehood.

Since May 15, 1948, was a Saturday, the Jews' holy Sabbath day, the newly organized Jewish nation instead declared its independence and statehood at 4:00 pm in the Tel Aviv Museum on May 14, 1948. After 2500 years of subjugation, persecution, exile, return, and the second dispersion, Israel was again a nation in its ancestral homeland. In one day, the land gave birth to the nation of Israel.

However, Israel's pain continued, just as Isaiah prophesied. The very next day, on May 15, 1948, the five nations surrounding Israel (Egypt, Jordan, Syria, Lebanon, and Iraq) initiated what would become her first major travail as a nation—the Israeli War of Independence. Israel would be greatly outmanned, outgunned, and out-financed, but God delivered them. Fifteen months after the fighting began, Israel defeated its neighbors, acquiring 6,000 square miles more territory than they had been allotted in UN Resolution 181.

The War of Independence wasn't the end of battles for Israel; it was just the beginning. Arab nations initiated the Egyptian War in 1956, Six-Day War in 1967, Yom Kippur War in 1973, three Lebanese wars, the Persian Gulf War, two intifadas (internal jihads and suicide bombings), tens of thousands of rocket firings from the Gaza Strip in 2012 and 2014, and an increase in individual stabbings by the Palestinians since 2015. These attacks have been the outcome of a people group bent on destroying Israel.

There are twenty-two Arab-controlled states in the world that joined together in 1945 to form The League of Arab States. One of the purposes in its charter is, "ridding that country [Palestine] of the Jews." At the peace accords in Khartoum, Sudan, after the Six-Day War in August 1967, the League of Arab States further declared, "No peace with Israel, no recognition of Israel, no negotiations with it."

Article 1 of their Palestinian Charter specifies that, "Palestine is the homeland of the Arab Palestinian people; it is an *indivisible part* (emphasis mine) of the Arab homeland." The Palestinian leaders have consistently declared that the land of Israel is Palestinian land so cannot be divided. Until the heart, attitude, teachings, leadership, and charter of the Arabs and Palestinians change, Israel will always travail—but God will deliver!

Just as God promised in Isaiah 66, Israel became a nation in one day through God's miraculous deliverance and in times of great distress. History documents seventeen miraculous victories during Israeli wars, most of them impossible by any other means but God. A DVD series entitled "Against All Odds, Israel Survives" testifies to miraculous stories from the beginning of Israeli statehood until modern times. The birth and nation of Israel is a modern-day miracle, a testament to the love and mercy of God.

Prophecy 8

ISRAEL'S RETURN TO ITS LAND COULD BE A SIGN THAT WE ARE IN THE FINAL GENERATION OF HISTORY

> Now learn the parable from the fig tree: when
> its branch has already become tender and puts
> forth its leaves, you know that summer is near;
> so, you too, when you see all these things, recog-
> nize that He is near, right at the door. Truly I say
> to you, this generation will not pass away until
> all these things take place. (Matthew 24:32–34)

I n Matthew 24, Jesus explains what signs will be evident in
the world leading up to His return. After providing a glimpse
into the moment of His return, Jesus shares the above parable
about the fig tree with his disciples. A parable is a story used
to illustrate a moral or spiritual lesson. In this case, Jesus uses
the fig tree to illustrate the timing of His return.

The Bible uses three specific trees as symbols for Israel:
the vine, the fig tree, and the olive tree. The vine is a symbol
of spiritual Israel as seen in Psalm 80:8–10: "You removed a
vine from Egypt; You drove out the nations and planted it. You
cleared the ground before it, and it took deep root and filled

the land. The mountains were covered with its shadow, and the cedars of God with its boughs."

The olive tree symbolizes Israel's and the Church's religious privileges in Romans 11:16–18:

> If the first piece of dough is holy, the lump is also; and if the root is holy, the branches are too. But if some of the branches were broken off, and you, being a wild olive, were grafted in among them and became partaker with them of the rich root of the olive tree, do not be arrogant toward the branches; but if you are arrogant, remember that it is not you who supports the root, but the root supports you.

The fig tree represents Israel's national privileges. We see this several places in the Bible. Jeremiah 24:5–7 states:

> Thus says the Lord God of Israel, "Like these good figs, so I will regard as good the captives of Judah, whom I have sent out of this place into the land of the Chaldeans. For I will set My eyes on them for good, and I will bring them again to this land; and I will build them up and not overthrow them, and I will plant them and not pluck them up. I will give them a heart to know Me, for I am the Lord; and they will be My people, and I will be their God, for they will return to Me with their whole heart."

Hosea 9:10 makes the point best, "I found Israel like grapes in the wilderness; I saw your forefathers as the earliest fruit on the fig tree in its first season." And Joel 1:7 explains that when a nation invaded Israel, "It has made My vine a waste and My fig tree splinters."

The fig tree is an unusual fruit-bearing tree because it produces two crops every year, with the first one appearing before the leaves sprout. The first crop, called the *breba*, grows early in the year on the old wood, below the beginning of the new leaf formation. These fruits are generally small, acidic, and inferior in texture and taste. Moving into the spring, the lush fig leaves begin to sprout on the new part of the branch, with new fruit popping up above these new leaves. The second crop of figs is juicy and edible by the fall.

With that groundwork laid, Jesus' use of the fig tree in Matthew 24 to represent Israel's fruitfulness may be giving us a glimpse into the general timing of His return. In watching a fig tree progress, the season of the year is apparent by the fruit and leaves on the tree. The 19th century Zionists may represent the first fig fruit who returned to Israel to prepare the land, so it "put forth its leaves." The new branch became tender (through the cultivation of the land) and eventually bore fruit (with the return of the Jews), symbolizing the establishment of the nation of Israel. Could Jesus be saying that He is right at the door, ready to return during the generation that sees Israel become a nation?

Finally, Jesus explains that the generation who would see the events of Matthew 24 would not die until He returns. Since the Baby Boomer generation (born between 1945 and 1964) has seen the beginning of the birth pangs that Jesus described in Matthew 24:8, as well as the rebirth of Israel, this could well be the final generation that will witness the return of Jesus Christ.

Prophecy 9

THE ISRAELI MILITARY WOULD BE A STRONG FORCE OF PROTECTION

In that day I will make the clans of Judah like
a firepot among pieces of wood and a flaming
torch among sheaves, so they will consume on
the right hand and on the left all the surrounding
peoples, while the inhabitants of Jerusalem
again dwell on their own sites in Jerusalem.
(Zechariah 12:6)

The context of Zechariah 12 is in "that day," the time surrounding the return of Jesus Christ when all the nations will be gathered against Jerusalem (Zechariah 12:3). In the passage above, Israel is described as being powerful enough to overcome its enemies. Israel's military might in the end times is more explicitly described in Ezekiel 37:10: "So I prophesied as He commanded me, and the breath came into them (Israel), and they came to life and stood on their feet, an exceedingly great army." The context is explaining how the "dry bones" of Israel were resurrected into a nation and a formidable force with whom to be reckoned.

When Zionists came to Palestine in the late 1800s, they anticipated a warm welcome because they were coming to rebuild the land. However, they often found themselves in disputes over property and water rights, thus requiring a form of protection from the Arab settlers. The first secret society called Bar-Giora was formed in 1907 to assist the pioneers. A few years later, Bar-Giora joined another group to form a new defensive organization called The Guild of Watchman. In 1920, a defensive military organized called Haganah, whose goals were to protect, train, produce, and smuggle weapons for the Jews. A more militant organization, Haganah-bet, was added to Haganah to provide offensive military support.

As Jewish colonists defended themselves against more aggressive violence, they realized the only way to gain their independence was to fight for it. In 1931 they formed Irgun Zvai Leumi (known as Irgun) as their national military organization to fight and defend against the Arabs and British. By 1940, splinter professional groups like the paramilitary fighters Lehi (aka the National Military Organization) and an elite fighting force known as Palmach were formed.

When Israel declared its independence in 1948, Israel needed to coordinate all of its military forces. Out of those groups, the Israeli Defense Force (IDF) was formed on May 31, 1948. The IDF includes the Israeli army, navy, and air force, which has defeated some of the mightiest armies in the Middle East. Today, the IDF has the fourth strongest military in the world.

Citizens of Israel are required to serve in the military, with a few exceptions such as religious objections. At the age of eighteen, men are drafted into the IDF for three years and women usually for two years. This opportunity serves to embolden the youth to understand their patriotic freedoms in Israel as well as prepare them to defend Israel for the rest of their lives. After completing their military service, each citizen is assigned to the IDF military reserve force to assist the military during times of emergency. Men can be called into service until age fifty-four and women until age thirty-eight. The IDF reserves can be activated within four hours of an emergency, even when communications are cut off.

Israel is one of only nine countries in the world that has nuclear capabilities. It is the largest manufacturer and exporter of drones. Israel is ranked number five of the twelve countries who have independent capabilities to launch reconnaissance satellites into orbit. Israel is the only country in the world with operational antiballistic missile defense systems on the national level: the Arrow system, the Iron Dome system, and David's Sling. It is currently working on a high-energy laser system to defend against medium-range rockets. Clearly, Israel has developed into a great and powerful military force.

Do you know why Israel is so advanced in their technology and military expertise? If it was not, it would not exist! Israel has not always been able to depend on arms or assistance from major western powers, so they were forced to develop their own defensive and offensive armaments. For example, on the eve of the 1948 War of Independence, Israel did not have a single cannon or tank. Its air force consisted of nine obsolete planes. The British and the United States imposed an arms embargo on them, forcing Israel to smuggle weapons into the country. Even with those restrictions, Israel prevailed. Without a strong military, the nations surrounding Israel would follow through with their promises to conquer Israel and exile the Jews.

Israel now calls itself the "Start-up Nation" because of all the advancements they have created technologically and militarily. They must be powerful enough to protect themselves because they cannot depend on anyone else—except God. Ultimately, God has promised, "Behold, He who keeps Israel will neither slumber nor sleep (Psalm 121:4).

Prophecy 10

ONCE ISRAEL CAME BACK TO THE LAND AFTER DISPERSION, GOD PROMISED NEVER AGAIN TO UPROOT THEM

Yes, I will cause men—My people Israel—
to walk on you and possess you, so that you
will become their inheritance and never again
bereave them of children. (Ezekiel 36:12)

The context of Ezekiel 36 is the return of the Jewish people to the land of Israel after their second and final dispersion. The passage uses a unique phrase to indicate that once the Jewish people have returned to their land a second time, they will never again be forced to leave it.

The Hebrew word for bereave is *sakol*, which means deprive or miscarry. God is promising the people Israel that upon their return from worldwide dispersion, the land would never again deprive them of Jewish children. The land would see the birth and life of Jewish children forever. No other nation would conquer this land again and uproot the Jewish people, though many would try.

In looking back through history, the Israelites, through Jacob and under God's direction, made a personal choice to leave their covenant land due to famine and move to Egypt (Genesis 46:1–6). As the Jews grew in numbers, they became a threat to the new pharaohs who chose to subjugate them to slave labor for 400 years, as prophesied by God in Genesis 15:14. Through the hand of Moses, God brought the Jews out of Egypt as a mighty nation of 600,000 men (Exodus 12:37) and eventually brought them back to their Promised Land. During this time, the Jews had neither been conquered by nor exiled to Egypt but, instead, had chosen of their own volition to move there. That was not the case with the next two exiles.

After the time of King Solomon, Israel was divided into two kingdoms. The northern kingdom of Israel was captured by Assyria in 722 BC. The southern kingdom of Judah would not be exiled until the nation of Babylon (which replaced Assyria) seized and destroyed Jerusalem between 605 and 586 BC. The Assyrian/Babylonian conquests had been prophesied by Isaiah, Jeremiah, Ezekiel, and other minor prophets. The people were in exile for seventy years (Jeremiah 25:9–11; Jeremiah 29:10) before they returned. When Persian King Cyrus conquered Babylon in 538 BC, he encouraged the Jews to return and repopulate their land (Ezra 1–3) exactly as God said would occur. This was the first exile of the Jews from their land and return to their land.

A decade after Israel returned from their first exile, God prophesied in Zechariah 7:14 that He would scatter the Jews a second time, but this time among the nations, when He said, "but I scattered them with a storm wind among all the nations whom they have not known. Thus the land is desolated behind them so that no one went back and forth, for they made the pleasant land desolate." Prophecies of this second worldwide dispersion can also be seen in Ezekiel 36:19 and Joel 3:2. As explained in previous prophecies, God also promised to return the Jews to their land after this second and final exile. But, did you know that God may have actually given the exact date of this return?

Grant R. Jeffrey, in his book *Armageddon, Appointment with Destiny*, explains how God accurately predicted 2600 years before that Israel would be reborn exactly on May 14, 1948. Jeffrey used Ezekiel 4:3–6 and Leviticus 26:18–28 to arrive at his conclusions. Ezekiel 4:3–6 reads:

> Then get yourself an iron plate and set it up as an iron wall between you and the city, and set your face toward it so that it is under siege, and besiege it. This is a sign to the house of Israel. As for you, lie down on your left side and lay the iniquity of the house of Israel on it; you shall bear their iniquity for the number of days that you lie on it. For I have assigned you a number of days corresponding to the years of their iniquity, three hundred and ninety days; thus you shall bear the iniquity of the house of Israel. When you have completed these, you shall lie down a second time, but on your right side and bear the iniquity of the house of Judah; I have assigned it to you for forty days, a day for each year.

This passage lays out a 430-year punishment for the Jewish nation because of their sins of rebellion and idolatry. As mentioned earlier, the Jews already suffered the seventy-year chastisement under the Babylonians, thus reducing the 430-year timeframe to 360 years. Leviticus 26:18 explains that the punishment must be multiplied by seven when it says, "If also after these things you do not obey Me, then I will punish you seven times more for your sins." If the calculations are correct, the Jews would have experienced 2,520 years of hardship between the two periods of exile.

Because the ancient Jewish calendar was based on a 360-day lunar calendar and the modern Gregorian calendar follows a solar calendar, this number was adjusted to 2,484 years. Based on this and additional assessments, Jeffrey concluded that from the end of the first exile in 586 BC to the end of the second exile on May 14, 1948 was exactly 2,484 years. While some may question Jeffrey's calculations, it is interesting to see how specific God is regarding His dealings with the Jewish people and their nation.

Now that the Israelites have been miraculously and prophetically returned to the land of their forefathers for the final time, God promised they would continue to be born there. These prophecies do not say there will be no wars, infighting, and struggles within the nation of Israel. Instead, He promised that no nation will ever completely conquer all of Israel again. Amos 9:14–15 reiterates that:

> Also I will restore the captivity of My people Israel, and they will rebuild the ruined cities and live in them; they will also plant vineyards and drink their wine, and make gardens and eat their fruit. I will also plant them on their land, and they will not again be rooted out from their land which I have given them.

Based on this promise, the Jewish people will remain in the land of Israel permanently from now on. The fulfillment of this prophecy has only been possible since 1948.

Prophecy 11

ALL JERUSALEM WOULD AGAIN BE GOVERNED BY THE JEWISH PEOPLE

In that day I will make the clans of Judah like a firepot among pieces of wood and a flaming torch among sheaves, so they will consume on the right hand and on the left all the surrounding peoples, while the inhabitants of Jerusalem again dwell on their own sites in Jerusalem. The Lord also will save the tents of Judah first, in order that the glory of the house of David and the glory of the inhabitants of Jerusalem will not be magnified above Judah. In that day the Lord will defend the inhabitants of Jerusalem. (Zechariah 12:6–8a)

Jerusalem is the holiest city for the Jews, their eternal capital, the location of their revered past temples and planned future temple, the area where their Messiah will come, and the place where the Messiah will reign on earth with His people. For Christians, it is also the place where Jesus gave His life to redeem us from our sins, where He rose from the dead to conquer death, and where He will return.

Jerusalem is mentioned 788 times in the New American Standard Bible (NASB) version of the Bible. It means "foundation of peace; peaceful possession." Jerusalem is the City of God (Psalm 48:1) where He has chosen to put His name (1 Kings 11:36). It is also known as the Mountain of God (Isaiah 56:7; Isaiah 65:25), Mount Moriah (2 Chronicles 3:1), My holy mountain (Psalm 2:6), Jebus (Joshua 15:8), Salem (Psalm 76:2; Hebrews 7:1–2), and Zion (2 Samuel 5:7; 1 Kings 8:1). The city has been known as Jerusalem since the time when Joshua brought the Israelites into the Promised Land (Joshua 10:1). When King David conquered the city in 1003 BC, he eventually built a house on the top of the southern slope and called that area the City of David. The first temple was later built by David's son Solomon above the City of David, on Mount Moriah, which is now called the Temple Mount. It was in this area where God dwelt with His people, making Jerusalem the most important city to the Jews from that time forward.

Jerusalem has been the center of Jewish existence and the capital of the Jewish people since the time of King David. It serves as historical proof of Jewish independence, sovereignty, nationality, and faith. Jerusalem is both a spiritual and a national symbol highlighting the unique eternal ties between God and the Jewish people, which has no parallel with any other nation. Jerusalem has never been the capital of another nation or people group.

While Jews have lived in or maintained a presence in Jerusalem for the past 3000 years, the city has not always been under Jewish control. After the Babylonians captured the city in 586 BC, Jerusalem fell under the authority of many other people groups prior to the establishment of the Jewish state of Israel in 1948.

When the United Nations General Assembly approved Resolution 181 on November 29, 1947 as a solution to divide up the land of Palestine as independent Arab and Jewish states, Jerusalem was designated a separate entity. It was not assigned as a part of either future independent state but was to be controlled by a special international regime. The residents of Jerusalem would automatically become "citizens of the City of Jerusalem," unless they chose citizenship in the Arab or Jewish state. When implementation of the partition plan failed due to Arab rejection and attack, control of Jerusalem was left in limbo.

Six months into the War of Independence, Israeli Lt. Colonel Moshe Dayan and Jordanian Lt. Colonel Abdullah Tal met to establish a "ceasefire" zone around Jerusalem, which effectively served as the boundaries between East Arab Jerusalem and West Israeli Jerusalem. This agreement was signed on November 30, 1948.

The Six-Day War in 1967 later changed those unofficial borders of Jerusalem. When that war began, Israeli leaders sent a message to King Hussein of Jordan, promising not to attack Jerusalem or the West Bank (Jordanian controlled land north and south of Jerusalem) if Jordan would stay out of this war. Jordan instead chose to use their strategic positions to attack Israelis. Israel responded by fighting and defeating the Jordanian forces in one day. On June 7, 1967, Defense Minister Moshe Dayan and his men captured the eastern section of Jerusalem. For the first time in 2500 years, Jerusalem was secured by the Jews as their undivided capital of Israel.

On that day, Moshe Dayan expressed Israel's purpose for securing Jerusalem when he said:

This morning, the Israel Defense Forces liberated Jerusalem. We have united Jerusalem, the divided capital of Israel. We have returned to the holiest of our holy places, never to part from it again. To our Arab neighbors we extend, also at this hour — and with added emphasis at this hour — our hand in peace. And to our Christian and Muslim fellow citizens, we solemnly promise full religious freedom and rights. We did not come to Jerusalem for the sake of other peoples' holy places, and not to interfere with the adherents of other faiths, but in order to safeguard its entirety, and to live there together with others, in unity. (http://www.mfa.gov.il/mfa/aboutisrael/state/jerusalem/pages/40th%20anniversary%20of%20the%20reunification%20of%20jerusalem.aspx)

Zechariah 12:6–8a notes the timing of the prophecy as "in that day," which refers to the period of time preceding and surrounding the return of Jesus Christ. At that time, Zechariah states Jerusalem will be inhabited and controlled by the descendants of Judah. God promised the same thing also in Zechariah 8:8, "I will bring them back and they will live in the midst of Jerusalem." The generation living at the time of the Six Day War in 1967 has seen the fulfillment of this prophecy after a 2500-year hiatus.

Prophecy 12

THE HEBREW LANGUAGE WOULD BE REVIVED

For then I will give to the peoples purified lips, that all of them may call on the name of the Lord, to serve Him shoulder to shoulder. (Zephaniah 3:9)

In the Hebrew language, the term *purified lips* from the passage above is translated more accurately as "pure language." The context of this passage indicates that God would again revive Hebrew, the Jews' holy language, after a time of extinction and before a time of spiritual revival.

Jewish tradition, as well as some Christian scholars, believe that Hebrew was the original language of man. Whether or not that is true, language changed when God "confused the language of the whole earth" and scattered the people (Genesis 11 — the Tower of Babel).

Abram (Abraham) was called a Hebrew (Genesis 14:13), meaning a son of Eber. The Old Testament was written primarily in the Hebrew language. Hebrew was the language spoken by the Jews throughout the centuries.

After the diaspora in the first and second centuries AD, Hebrew was relegated to the language used in synagogues and Yeshivas (religious schools) for teaching and reading the Torah. Everyday Jews spoke Greek or Latin or adopted the language of the countries in which they resided. Jews in Europe later mixed Hebrew with German to create a new language called Yiddish. In the western Mediterranean Basin, Jews mixed Hebrew with Spanish, thus developing a Ladino slang. About eighteen "Jewish" languages have been derived from the original Hebrew, most of which are extinct.

As Zionism was gaining popularity in the 1800s, a young prodigy named Eliezer Yitzhak Perlman (1858–1922) from Belarus was taught at any early age to read Hebrew. After he celebrated his Bar Mitzvah at age thirteen, he was sent to a Yeshiva where he was introduced to Hebrew both as a holy language and a secular language. Eliezer became a Zionist with a passion to see the Jews return to their homeland and restore his beloved Hebrew as their native language. He later wrote, "I have decided that in order to have our own land and political life, it is also necessary that we have a language to hold us together. That language is Hebrew."

Eliezer changed his name to Eliezer Ben-Yehuda, which means "son of Yehudi." Yehuda was the Hebrew translation of his father's name but was also the Hebrew word for "Judea," representing his beloved Israel. He married, moved to Jerusalem, spoke only Hebrew, educated his family only in Hebrew, trained the locals in this language, and dedicated his life to restoring the Hebrew language to everyday life.

Ben-Yehuda spent most of his time searching for ancient Hebrew words and examples of their usage. He scoured libraries throughout the Middle East and Europe, researching over 40,000 books and accumulating 450,000 notes on ancient Hebrew words. He began writing his Hebrew dictionary that would ultimately be finished after his death by his wife and son, Hemda and Ehud. They worked with linguistics experts to complete the seventeen-volume Hebrew dictionary in 1958.

About the time he had published his first five volumes in 1922, his work had received worldwide acclaim. His greatest victory came in 1921 when the British government recognized three official languages for Palestine: English, Arabic, and

Hebrew. Postage stamps were issued in Hebrew for the first time ever, anywhere in the world.

The ancient Hebrew language, extinct for nearly 2000 years, was resurrected by Eliezer Ben-Yehuda and recognized by the Zionist Organization in 1928 as the official language for those returning to Israel.

Today, Hebrew is the official language in Israel, along with Arabic. The revival of this dead language by a once-dispersed nation is unique in human history yet matches with God's prophecy to provide the Jews a pure language in these last days.

Prophecy 13

THE SHEKEL WOULD AGAIN BECAME THE MONETARY UNIT OF ISRAEL

And the shekel shall be twenty gerahs: twenty shekels, five and twenty shekels, fifteen shekels, shall be your maneh. All the people of the land shall give this oblation for the prince in Israel. (Ezekiel 45:12, 16)

The prophecy of Ezekiel 45 will occur after the Messiah has returned to earth, has established His long awaited kingdom on earth, and has taken His seat as King of kings and Lord of lords in the temple in Jerusalem. When that occurs, the shekel will be the monetary unit in Israel. In reality, the shekel is in use in Israel today.

The shekel was the monetary unit and a unit of weight used by the nations and the Jews throughout the Old Testament (Genesis 23:15). It is last mentioned in Scripture in Matthew 17:27 when Jesus told Peter to use the shekel found in the mouth of the fish to pay the tax. History records that the Jewish Zealots of AD 66–70, and later the Jews of the Bar-Kochba revolt in AD 132–135, considered it their source of currency. After that, the shekel became extinct.

Shekels are again being used in Israel as their monetary unit, just as the Bible said they would be by the time the Messiah returns. The shekel replaced the Israeli lira or pound in 1980. The New Israeli shekel (NIS) replaced the original shekel in 1985 and is still in use. It is divided into ten agoras, much like the dollar is divided into ten dimes. Generally, the exchange rate between shekels and dollars is a little less than four shekels to $1, though this fluctuates with the rise and fall of both currencies.

The revitalization of the shekel as the financial currency in Israel has already occurred and is another fulfilled prophecy pointing to the return of Jesus Christ.

Prophecy 14

THE JEWISH TEMPLE WILL BE REBUILT

> Then there was given me a measuring rod like
> a staff; and someone said, "Get up and measure
> the temple of God and the altar, and those who
> worship in it. Leave out the court which is out-
> side the temple and do not measure it, for it has
> been given to the nations; and they will tread
> under foot the holy city for forty-two months."
> (Revelation 11:1–2)

The importance of the Jewish temple cannot be overstated, either historically or for the future. The temple is the house where God chose to dwell with His people and to place His name forever (2 Kings 21:7b). And, it is the place where the Messiah will reign for one thousand years as "King of kings, and Lord of lords" (Revelation 19:16).

The precursor to the permanent temple in Jerusalem was the portable tabernacle (also known as the tent of meeting) erected in the wilderness. When the Israelites departed Egypt, they went to Mount Sinai to worship God. It was there that God gave Moses the Ten Commandments and other directives by which the Jews were to live. He also gave Moses specific instructions on the building of the tabernacle, its instruments, and the priestly garments needed for service and sacrifice in the tabernacle. It was in the tabernacle that God would dwell among His people. Exodus 29:44–46 explains:

> I will consecrate the tent of meeting and the altar; I will also consecrate Aaron and his sons to minister as priests to Me. I will dwell among the sons of Israel and will be their God. They shall know that I am the Lord their God who brought them out of the land of Egypt, that I might dwell among them; I am the Lord their God.

After the tent of meeting was constructed, Exodus 40:34 confirms, "Then the cloud covered the tent of meeting, and the glory of the Lord filled the tabernacle."

God dwelt with the Jews, via the tabernacle, throughout their forty years in the wilderness and during their first centuries in the Promised Land. The Bible even calls the tabernacle the "temple of the Lord" (1 Samuel 1:9) when it was housed first in Gilgal and later in Shiloh, about thirty miles north of Jerusalem, for 369 years. After Shiloh, the tabernacle was located in various cities until King David brought it with much rejoicing and dancing to the City of David in Jerusalem, according to 2 Samuel 6:12–15.

King David's desire was to build a permanent house for the Lord in Jerusalem (2 Samuel 7:2). However, God explained that the house of the Lord would be built by David's son, King Solomon (2 Samuel 7:13).

Solomon built the first temple in 966 BC on Mount Moriah in Jerusalem. That was the exact same location where Abraham had been willing to offer his son Isaac on the altar before the Lord (Genesis 22), where David later erected an altar to the Lord at the threshing floor of Araunah (2 Samuel 24), where Solomon built the first temple (1 Chronicles 3:1), and where the second temple was built (Ezra 3). It was here that God dwelt among His people.

When Solomon dedicated the temple, he and all Israel worshipped, prayed, and offered 142,000 animals in sacrifice to the Lord. The glory of the Lord filled the house (2 Chronicles 7:1). God appeared to Solomon and explained the importance for Israel to walk in His ways (2 Chronicles 7:12–22), which they agreed to do. Solomon's temple was destroyed in 586 BC when the Babylonians conquered Jerusalem, burned the temple, and exiled most Jews to Babylon.

When the Persian King Cyrus conquered the Babylonian Empire, he encouraged the exiled Jews to return to their land and rebuild God's house in Jerusalem (Ezra 1). Nearly 50,000 Jews returned in 538 BC and started fourteen months later to rebuild the temple (Ezra 2). Due to opposition, construction ceased for nearly twenty years, but the second temple (also known as Zerubbabel's temple and later as Herod's temple) was finally completed in 515 BC.

Over the centuries the temple fell into disrepair. Around 18 BC, King Herod began to refurbish the temple foundation, structure and outside courts; a project that would not be totally completed until AD 64. All of this was built on a flattened surface, totaling approximately 35 acres, and supported by retaining walls all around. The area came to be known as the Temple Mount. In AD 70, this second temple and the city of Jerusalem were destroyed by the Romans.

Leading up to the destruction of the city and the sanctuary in AD 70, Roman procurator Gessius Florus ruled Judea with a strong arm. He had no sympathies for the Jewish traditions or their holy temple, so he seized silver from the temple for taxes. When an uproar ensued, he sent troops into Jerusalem and massacred 3,600 citizens in AD 66. These actions sparked a rebellion, the First Jewish Revolt, throughout Israel. To nip this rebellion in the bud, Emperor Nero commissioned Cestius Gallus, who was the Roman governor of the region, to attack. He marched from Syria with 20,000 soldiers, besieged Jerusalem for six months, yet failed to capture it. Six thousand Roman soldiers died. The Jews confiscated their weapons.

Emperor Nero then rallied Vespasian, a decorated Roman general, to end the Jewish rebellion. He conquered the territories on all sides of Jerusalem before besieging Jerusalem itself. Before he could capture the city, Emperor Nero died, and Vespasian returned to Rome to be crowned emperor. One of his first imperial acts was to appoint his son Titus to end the Jewish Revolt once and for all. This was completed in Jerusalem in AD 70 and finalized at Masada in AD 73, with the Jews either killed or taken into slavery to Rome. Titus celebrated that victory by having the Arch of Titus built in the Roman Forum in Rome. The Arch depicts Jewish captives carrying a menorah and other artifacts to Rome.

When Jerusalem was conquered, the Jewish temple was completely destroyed. According to Josephus, the Jewish historian at that time, Titus wanted to preserve the magnificent temple, but his soldiers burned it to the ground while fighting the last of the Jews. Jesus prophesied this would occur in Matthew 24:1–2: "Jesus came out from the temple and was going away when His disciples came up to point out the temple buildings to Him. And He said to them, 'Do you not see all these things? Truly I say to you, not one stone here will be left upon another, which will not be torn down.'"

With the destruction of the temple, the Jews had no place to offer sacrifices or conduct their formal worship. During their exile to Babylon 600 years earlier, they adjusted their worship by meeting in community centers called synagogues for prayer, worship, and reading of the Torah. They continued this practice when they returned by building synagogues in Israel even though the temple was where the Jewish feasts were celebrated. These synagogues would become the only places of worship after the temple was destroyed in AD 70. The few Jews who remained in Israel after the destruction of Jerusalem moved their religious activity and their educational institutions first to Jamnia and later to Sepphoris, without ever again offering sacrifices.

According to a prophetic passage in the book of Daniel, however, those sacrifices will be initiated again before the Messiah returns. Daniel 9:24–27 contains some foundational prophecies and future time periods concerning Israel known as the seventy weeks of Daniel. For now we will focus on Daniel 9:27, which reads in part, "And he will make a firm covenant with the many for one week, but in the middle of the week he will put a stop to sacrifice and grain offering." In order for the sacrifices to be stopped, there must be sacrifices in the first place. Sacrifices can only be offered on the temple grounds, which indicates a temple will again be built on the same site as previous temples. John also confirms the existence of this future temple when he is told to measure it in Revelation 11:1–2.

Ezekiel 40–48 provides detailed dimensions of the future temple where the Messiah will reign. According to Ezekiel 43:1–5, the glory of the Lord will return to the house through the eastern gate. It is possible this is the same temple referred to in Daniel 9 and Revelation 11, or it may be yet another temple prepared specifically for the reign of Jesus Christ on earth.

It is absolutely impossible right now for a Jewish temple to be built on the Temple Mount because the Jordanian Muslim Waqf has authority on that Temple Mount, even though Israel controls the territory. The Muslims do not recognize Israel's historic or religious right to the Temple Mount, seldom let Jews on the Temple Mount, and control the two mosques currently on the site. They have made it clear they will *never* allow Israel to have any structures built on the Temple Mount. However, with God, all things are possible. He has said it will happen, so it will!

An organization in Jerusalem called the Temple Institute is "dedicated to all aspects of the Divine commandment for Israel to build a house for G-d's presence, the Holy Temple, on Mount Moriah in Jerusalem." Having visited the Temple Institute several times, we have seen the holy instruments that have already been prepared for worship and sacrifice in this new temple.

The Levitical priests have been determined through DNA and their priestly garments sewn. The Temple Institute has recently developed The Nezer HaKodesh Institute for Kohanic Studies where the priests are learning and practicing the rituals for temple service. Everything is ready to start building a new temple, once the Temple Mount is available to them.

Many groups in Israel have formed in an attempt to secure at least part of the Temple Mount for a future temple site and to begin offering sacrifices there. One such group is the modern day Sanhedrin (called the Council in Matthew 26:59) that was formed in October 2004. Seventy-one Orthodox Jewish rabbis claim to be renewing this ancient Jewish religious high court, which existed until AD 358. They even offered a symbolic sacrifice on a specially built altar at Givat Hananya, which overlooks the Temple Mount.

In an even more unique way to regain Jewish control over the Temple Mount, a private foundation representing the descendants of King David recently launched a lawsuit, presenting a legal claim to ownership of the Temple Mount. They cited 2 Samuel 24:24–25 as evidence that King David purchased the site, with no one else proving legal claim to it since then. Therefore, the Temple Mount should have legally been passed down to King David's male descendants as their inheritance.

While I highly doubt the recent activities by the Sanhedrin or other groups fulfill the prophecies above, they do prove the interest by the religious Jewish community to build the new temple and to once again perform the ancient rituals at the temple. They have prepared all the research, articles, clothing, utensils, and resources necessary for a new temple, enabling one to be built and furnished within months of receiving approval to do so. At this time, the temple and the sacrificial system have not yet been instituted. But, based on the biblical prophecies, they will be prior to the return of Jesus Christ.

Prophecy 15

A PUREBRED RED HEIFER MUST BE FOUND TO CLEANSE THE TEMPLE MOUNT

This is the statute of the law which the Lord
has commanded, saying, "Speak to the sons of
Israel that they bring you an unblemished red
heifer in which is no defect and on which a yoke
has never been placed... Now a man who is
clean shall gather up the ashes of the heifer and
deposit them outside the camp in a clean place,
and the congregation of the sons of Israel shall
keep it as water to remove impurity; it is purification from sin." (Numbers 19:2, 9)

Holy cow! A red heifer as mentioned in the passage above
is exactly what is necessary to purify the Temple Mount
before the third temple can be built. Is there one available?

Purification is a fundamental ritual in the Jewish traditions,
whether it be through the ritual baths called *mikvehs*, washing
of hands or purification from sin by water infused with the
ashes of the red heifer (*parah adumah* in Hebrew). Once a

person or area is deemed unclean, it must be purified before it can be used again for the Lord.

Therefore, prior to building the third temple, the Temple Mount must first be cleansed from impurities. That can only occur by using the ashes of an unblemished red heifer mixed with water as explained in Numbers 19. The red heifer must meet these additional physical criteria and must be sacrificed in a certain way to meet the biblical and traditional requirements:

- female heifer, completely red, without blemish, no defect
- two single hairs not red disqualifies it
- kept under strict care until it reaches three years old
- never put to work
- no leaning, riding, putting cloth on its back
- never having been mated

According to the Temple Institute in Jerusalem, the Mishna (oral tradition of Jewish law) teaches that from the beginning of the red heifer purification system explained in Numbers 19 until the destruction of the second temple in AD 70, a total of only nine red heifers had been sacrificed for their ashes. For nearly 2000 years they have been awaiting the tenth red heifer, which the rabbis believe will occur in association with the Messianic era.

God can provide this rare, pure red heifer to meet the Jewish requirements of purification. Or, perhaps man through scientific means will produce the perfect sacrificial cow. For decades now, ranchers and breeders have been attempting to help with the fulfillment of prophecy by creating the perfect animal through inbreeding and embryo transplants. Many heifers were sited and certified perfect by rabbis, only to later be determined unclean. The eight dates and locations that follow show the international interest of people who tried to produce, and thought they had found, the red heifer. This shows how close Israel is to discovering the one animal needed to purify the temple before it can be rebuilt. No other generation has been this close to seeing the birth of a biblical red heifer.

1990s—Clyde Lott in Mississippi (bred and shipped red heifers to Israel)
1997—Kfar Hasidim, Israel
2002—United States
2002—Israel
2014—United States
2015—Negev Desert, Israel
2017—Baja, Mexico
2017—West Virginia, United States

According to an *Arutz Sheva 7* article on December 7, 2015 entitled "Temple Institute Raising A Genuise Red Heifer," the Temple Institute is partnering with an expert Israeli rancher to raise a herd of red heifers for use in the Third Temple.

> In order for a Red Heifer to be considered kosher for use, it must be raised from birth in Israel under specific conditions and in a controlled environment … During antiquity, Israelites waited for the birth of a potential Red Heifer, but with a combination of Torah knowledge and advanced science, The Temple Institute believes a Red Heifer can be bred in our modern times. Under the guidance of Temple Institute rabbis, frozen embryos of Red Angus cattle will be implanted into domestic cattle in Israel, leading to the introduction of this breed into the Jewish state. This method, authorized by Israel's Agriculture Ministry, has already proved successful with the birth of a number of male Red Angus.

While Numbers 19 explains the significance of the red heifer for purification of sin, it also foreshadows Jesus Christ who purifies us. The heifer's blood purified the tabernacle while Christ's blood purifies us from sin. As the heifer was without blemish, so is Jesus. As the cow was sacrificed outside the camp, Jesus was sacrificed outside the city. We see this comparison in Hebrews 9:13–14, "For if the blood of goats and bulls and the ashes of a heifer sprinkling those who have been defiled sanctify for the cleansing of the flesh, how much more will the blood of Christ, who through the eternal Spirit offered Himself without blemish to God, cleanse your conscience from dead works to serve the living God?"

Since the Jews follow law and tradition, rather than a belief in Jesus Christ, they must secure a red heifer that matches biblical standards in order to purify the Temple Mount before building the next temple. Whether it be through science, technology, or the providential hand of God, this unique animal must be certified Kosher (meeting Jewish requirements). The current generation has been the first to see this possibility since the time of Christ. It could happen at any time.

Prophecy 16

THE PRIESTLY TRIBE OF LEVI MUST BE IDENTIFIED TO SERVE IN THE TEMPLE

> Bring the tribe of Levi near and set them before Aaron the priest, that they may serve him. They shall perform the duties for him and for the whole congregation before the tent of meeting, to do the service of the tabernacle... Now, behold, I have taken the Levites from among the sons of Israel instead of every firstborn, the first issue of the womb among the sons of Israel. So the Levites shall be Mine. (Numbers 3:6, 7, 12)

God chose Moses' brother Aaron and his descendants to serve as high priests before God (Exodus 28). He also appointed the tribe of Levi to be set apart as priests to perform the duties in the tabernacle and temple (Numbers 3). The priests and high priests were the only ones allowed into the tabernacle and temple. In order to follow the biblical law, only these priestly Levites will be allowed to serve in the third temple. Therefore, these Kohanim (Jewish priests) must be identified.

When the second temple was destroyed, all the Jewish records were also destroyed, making it impossible to determine the priestly inheritance. It has been believed for centuries that the name Cohen was a derivative of Kohanim, making them of priestly lineage. Now that supposition can be proven through DNA.

The Cohen hypothesis was first tested by Professor Karl Skorecki, himself a Kohen, at the Rambam-Technion Medical Center in Haifa, Israel in 1997. Testing for two distinct Y chromosome markers (YAP and DYS 19), labeling it the J1 Cohen Modal Haplotype, a particular genetic marker on the Y chromosome (YAP) was detected in 98.5 percent of the Kohanim, and in a significantly lower percentage of non-Kohanim Jews.

Now that these Kohanim have been identified, they must be trained in priestly service. Almost one hundred years ago, Jerusalem's Chief Rabbi Kook established Torat Kohanim, a yeshiva (school for Orthodox rabbinic studies) designed for the training of Levites to serve in a rebuilt temple. His training has continued at the Third Temple Academy established in 2009 in Mitzpe Yericho, a short drive east of Jerusalem on the road to Jericho. The priests receive hands-on training at a replica of the third temple. They have performed dress rehearsals for the daily service in the temple and an authentic reenactment of the Korban Pesach (Passover offering).

The priestly garments, including the high priest's breastplate, the items in the temple, the musical instruments of the Levitical choir and the articles necessary for temple service have been recreated by the Temple Institute in Jerusalem.

It was in 1953 when the first DNA module was first mapped out. It became sophisticated enough for criminal investigations in 1986. Now it can and has been used to match paternity, ancestry, and all aspects of identification. It is in God's perfect timing that this instrument is available to determine the legitimate Levitical priests for temple service. Another prophecy fulfilled!

Prophecy 17

ISRAEL WILL SEEK PEACE BUT THERE WILL BE NO PEACE

> For you yourselves know full well that the day of the Lord will come just like a thief in the night. While they are saying, "Peace and safety!" then destruction will come upon them suddenly like labor pains upon a woman with child, and they will not escape. (1 Thessalonians 5:2–3)

For one hundred years, Israel has worked diligently to establish a nation that would live peacefully side-by-side with their neighbors. From the Balfour Declaration in 1917 to Israeli Prime Minister Netanyahu's willingness to negotiate with the Palestinians in 2017, there have been no less than thirty peace agreements signed between Israel and others. Unfortunately, most of Israel's concessions have been met with noncompliance and escalating violence. No matter what Israel offers, that permanent peace continues to elude them.

Prophecy 6 outlined many opportunities offered the Jewish and the Arab peoples to develop two states living peacefully alongside each other. In each situation, the Jews agreed to the land partitions, but the Arabs did not. Instead of accepting peace, the Arabs consistently started a war or *intifada*.

Since Israel became a nation in 1948, it has defended its sovereignty in over a dozen wars perpetrated by its neighbors as well as internal terrorism carried out by individual Arabs:

1948 War of Independence
1956 War with Egypt
1967 Six Day War
1973 Yom Kippur War
1982 Palestinian war from south Lebanon
1987–91 First Palestinian Intifada (shaking off)
1991 Persian Gulf War (Iraq)
1996 Hezbollah in Lebanon
2000–05 Second Palestinian Intifada
2006 Hezbollah in Lebanon
2008, 2012, 2014 Hamas rocket wars from Gaza

In the Oslo Accords orchestrated by former President Bill Clinton and agreed to by Israeli Prime Minister Yitzhak Rabin and Palestinian Chairman Yasser Arafat in 1993, a "land for peace" agreement was finally reached. In this "Roadmap for Peace," Israel would gradually give autonomy to areas primarily occupied by Palestinians (Gaza Strip, Bethlehem, Hebron, Nablus, etc.) in exchange for peace with them. As the details for the "Roadmap for Peace" were established between 1993 and 2001, six separate agreements were signed between Israel and the Palestinian Authority. In each case, Israel complied, but the Palestinians defaulted on their promises.

In one of those agreements, Israel relinquished complete control of the Gaza Strip to the Palestinian Authority in what was supposed to be the beginning of a Palestinian state. The Palestinians could have built the Gaza Strip into a "Singapore of the Middle East" but chose instead to become a depressed state, with over 41 percent unemployment and a hotbed for terrorism against Israel.

In 2000 and again in 2008, the prime ministers of Israel offered peace agreements to the Palestinian Authority providing

97 percent of the West Bank land they wanted for a state, with East Jerusalem for their capital. The Palestinians rejected both offers.

The early leaders in the Zionism movement realized that the Jews could only live in peace if they lived in a land of their own. They have lived in their own state for seventy years now but have not achieved that elusive peace. Why? As explained previously, the Palestinians are not willing to share the land of Israel. The Palestinians refuse to recognize the nation of Israel, to the point that all their maps show that land as the state of Palestine instead of the internationally recognized state of Israel.

Israel has learned that the best way to achieve peace is to help their neighbors with new technology that will improve their countries. Israel has provided agricultural expertise to Jordan, which is using it to grow crops down the Jordan River Valley. Israel collaborates with their Sunni Muslim neighbors in military options to protect those neighbors from their Shia Muslim adversaries. However, those alliances can shift at any time as they have in the past. When they do, Israel will find itself isolated from much of the world.

Since peace is Israel's number one priority, it is not surprising that the Bible predicts an agreement will be made with Israel in the last days. According to Daniel 9:27, Israel will be coerced into accepting a seven-year covenant with the future world leader (known as the Antichrist). But, it will be short lived, only three and a half years, before the Antichrist breaks it.

The prospect of the Jews living in a peaceful state has only been possible since they became a nation in 1948. Since then, they have been calling for peace, yet there has been no peace, just as has been prophesied. True peace will only come to Israel when the Prince of Peace returns, and the world bows in submission to Him.

Prophecy 18

ISRAEL'S NEIGHBORS WILL FIGHT TO DESTROY THE NATION OF ISRAEL

For behold, Your enemies make an uproar, and those who hate You have exalted themselves. They make shrewd plans against Your people, and conspire together against Your treasured ones. They have said, "Come, and let us wipe them out as a nation, that the name of Israel be remembered no more." For they have conspired together with one mind; against You they make a covenant: the tents of Edom and the Ishmaelites, Moab and the Hagrites; Gebal and Ammon and Amalek, Philistia with the inhabitants of Tyre; Assyria also has joined with them; they have become a help to the children of Lot. (Psalm 83:2–8)

Jumpin' Jehoshaphat! Could a psalm written 3000 years ago have prophetic significance for this generation? Let's do some investigation to find out.

Who wrote the psalms? Most would answer that King David wrote them. Actually, only half of the psalms are attributed to him. Other psalmists included Asaph (12), sons of Korah (11),

73

Solomon (2), Heman (1), Moses (1), Ethan the Ezrahite (1), and forty-eight anonymous authors. Psalm 83 was penned by Asaph. Asaph was a Levite appointed by King David as a worship minister to thank and praise the Lord God of Israel before the Ark of the Lord (I Chronicles 16:4–5). He was also a seer, one who prophesied under the direction of the king (1 Chronicles 25:2; 2 Chronicles 29:30). It is not surprising then that this author would provide a prophecy into Israel's future.

To understand this prophecy, these enemies of Israel described in Psalm 83:6–8 must be identified. Charts 1 and 2 at the beginning of this book outline the ancient and modern countries surrounding Israel that are named in Psalm 83. Has there ever been a war in Israel encompassing those people groups?

Some people believe the miraculous victory experienced through King Jehoshaphat in 2 Chronicles 20 resembles the people groups and situation mentioned in Psalm 83. However, the nations outlined in 2 Chronicles 20 are only a few of the ones listed in Psalm 83. Technically, no passage of Scripture matches with the specific details of Psalm 83 as having been fulfilled in the past.

In modern times, however, there was a very important war that included all these nations. When UN Resolution 181 was approved on November 29, 1947, it recommended the creation of both Jewish and Arab states according to specifically designated borders. Israel accepted Resolution 181 and declared statehood on May 14, 1948. The Arabs did not.

On, May 15, 1948, the five Arab nations surrounding Israel went to war with Israel. Those nations included Egypt, Transjordan, Syria, Iraq, and Lebanon, with finances and behind-the-scenes support from Saudi Arabia. Does that sound familiar? It should, as these are the nations mentioned in Psalm 83:6–8. Their goal was to wipe out Israel as a nation, so Israel would be remembered no more. Again, that sounds familiar as it was the stated purpose for war in Psalm 83:4.

When the fighting ended on July 20, 1949, Israel emerged with the land borders designated by UN Resolution 181, plus about 60 percent of the area proposed for the Arab state. It was humiliating for the more populous and stronger Arab countries to be defeated by this new, fledgling Jewish state. Yet, Psalm 83:13–17 said it would happen.

Then, in 1967, a similar war broke out with all the nations listed in Psalm 83, except Lebanon. The result was even more devastating for the Arabs when Israel captured 100 percent of the land originally partitioned for the Arab state, in addition to the Sinai Peninsula and the Golan Heights. If Lebanon was involved in an indirect manner, this too could have fulfilled Psalm 83.

Even with the possible modern-day fulfillment of the Psalm 83 prophecy, many Bible prophecy scholars believe Psalm 83 is still to be fulfilled. Since these nations have worked together over the past seventy years, they could certainly coalesce again to war against Israel in a yet-future battle. If this is a war that will occur in the future, it will result in an unprecedented victory for Israel, resulting in greater territorial expansion into these countries. Only time will tell if this a future prophecy.

It is important to consider that Psalm 83 may not have been written as a future prophecy at all. Most passages designate the timing of the end times prophecies using phrases such as "Day of the Lord" or "last days" to designate them as future prophecies. Nowhere in Psalm 83 does it state the timing of its fulfillment. In addition, there is no outcome explained in Psalm 83 as there is in most other prophecies.

It is no coincidence that all these nations are on the scene today, with the same coordinated intent to destroy Israel as explained in Psalm 83. Perhaps we have already seen the fulfillment of Psalm 83 in this generation, or perhaps it will be fulfilled in the near future. Either way, God has clearly established these nations in their locations for such a time as this.

Prophecy 19

JERUSALEM WOULD BE A DIVIDED CITY

> Behold, a day is coming for the Lord when the
> spoil taken from you will be divided among you.
> For I will gather all the nations against Jerusalem
> to battle, and the city will be captured, the houses
> plundered, the women ravished and half of the
> city exiled, but the rest of the people will not be
> cut off from the city. (Zechariah 14:1–2)

There is some disagreement among scholars as to whether this prophecy was fulfilled during the War of Independence in 1948 or if it will be fulfilled shortly before the return of Christ. It is possible that this could be one of those prophecies that has a dual fulfillment: one prophecy with two fulfillments at two different times.

Some biblical prophecies have a near fulfillment and then, later, a future fulfillment. For example, Isaiah prophesied in Isaiah 7:14–16:

> Therefore the Lord Himself will give you a sign:
> Behold, a virgin will be with child and bear a
> son, and she will call His name Immanuel. He
> will eat curds and honey at the time He knows

enough to refuse evil and choose good. For before the boy will know enough to refuse evil and choose good, the land whose two kings you dread will be forsaken.

The immediate context of this passage referred to the birth of Isaiah's son. Before that son would be very old, Assyria would conquer the two kings from Israel and Syria. History proves that occurred in 722 BC. In addition, Matthew 1:23 quotes Isaiah 7:14 in prophesying to Joseph that Mary would bear a son, Jesus, also known as Immanuel, God with us. The angel Gabriel made a similar announcement to Mary in Luke 1:31–35 that as a virgin, she would conceive a Son, Jesus, when the Holy Spirit came upon her and the power of the Highest overshadowed her. So the one prophecy from Isaiah 7:14 had a past fulfillment near the time the prophecy was made and a future fulfillment over seven hundred years later.

The prophecy from Zechariah 14:1–2 mentions the division of Jerusalem. Zechariah wrote this prophecy after the return of the exiles from Persia in the early 6th century BC. From that time until the 20th century, Jerusalem has been conquered and destroyed, as the Romans did in AD 70, but never divided with half the city exiled.

After Israel declared its independence on May 14, 1948, the surrounding Arab nations attacked the new country. It was imperative that the Jews protect their capital city, Jerusalem. They were able to hold off the enemy for only six months before it became apparent the city was hopelessly divided. On November 30, 1948, Lt. Colonel Moshe Dayan, Commander of the Israeli Etzioni Brigade, and Lt. Colonel Abdullah Tal, the Jordanian Commander, met to work out a temporary agreement as to the general boundaries of Jerusalem.

It was determined at the meeting that Israel would govern West Jerusalem. The Kingdom of Jordan would control the eastern half of the city, including the Old City with the Temple

Mount. With Jordanian possession of East Jerusalem, Jewish residents were forced from their East Jerusalem homes, Jews were not allowed to visit the Wailing Wall or the Temple Mount, fifty-eight synagogues in that area were destroyed, and the Jewish cemetery on the Mount of Olives was desecrated and plundered.

When the War of Independence ended in July of 1949, Jerusalem was still divided. It remained so for nineteen years until Israel liberated the city during the Six Day War on June 7, 1967. The fences and concrete walls dividing the streets and neighborhoods were torn down and the mines were removed. The entire city was consolidated under the Israeli Jerusalem Municipality with authority over the Temple Mount maintained by the Jordanian Waqf. Even though Israel now governs all of Jerusalem, the Arabs continue to claim East Jerusalem as the capital of their future Palestinian state.

During the war in which Jerusalem was divided, all the nations surrounding Israel went to battle, captured the eastern half of the city, plundered the houses, killed men and women, exiled Jews from the eastern half the city but left the western part of Jerusalem to the Jews. You can see how much of the Zechariah prophecy was fulfilled in 1948. That could mean the prophecy has already been fulfilled. However, not all the nations of the world fought against Jerusalem in 1948, which means the 1948 division could have been a partial fulfillment of the prophecy with a future fulfillment occurring before Jesus returns. If the Israelis and Palestinians reach a peace agreement, it could include dividing Jerusalem again with similar results as occurred in 1948.

> If I forget you, O Jerusalem, may my right hand forget her skill. (Psalm 137:5)

Prophecy 20

TURKEY, RUSSIA, AND IRAN WILL FORM AN ALLIANCE TO WAR AGAINST ISRAEL

> Son of man, set your face toward Gog of the land of Magog, the prince of Rosh, Meshech and Tubal (and Persia, Ethiopia and Put... Gomer, Beth-togarmah—vs. 6–7) and prophesy against him... After many days you will be summoned; in the latter years you will come into the land that is restored from the sword, whose inhabitants have been gathered from many nations to the mountains of Israel which had been a continual waste; but its people were brought out from the nations, and they are living securely, all of them. You will go up, you will come like a storm; you will be like a cloud covering the land, you and all your troops, and many peoples with you. (Ezekiel 38:2, 8)

Gobble, Gobble! If Turkey, Russia, Iran, Libya, and Sudan have their way, they will gobble up Israel in the latter days before the return of Christ.

One of the most infamous end times wars is the Gog and Magog War as outlined in Ezekiel 38 and 39. A coalition headed by a prince known as Gog from the land of Magog (former Scythia—modern Russia), Rosh, Meshech, and Tubal (modern Turkey) will join forces with troops from Gomer, Beth-togarmah (eastern Turkey), Persia (Iran), Ethiopia (Northern Sudan), and Put (Libya). Never has a coalition or a war like this ever occurred since Ezekiel wrote this prophecy in the 6th century BC. It is important to look at the current position of each of these countries to see if it is possible that this prophecy might be fulfilled soon.

Russia

While Russia has been in existence for centuries, it has only been in the last few centuries that Russia has gained international prominence. During and after World War I, the Russian government suffered a crisis of confidence resulting in chaos, civil war, the Bolshevik revolution, and ultimately, a new communist government headed by one of the most ruthless dictators of all times, Joseph Stalin. Stalin is believed to have orchestrated the murder of over 40 million people during his 1922–1952 reign, as he established Russia as a socialist country.

Since then, we have seen the rise, fall, and rise again of Russia on the international scene. Russia is a partner with most rogue nations as well as many western powers in trade, weaponry, and oil. They have been flexing their muscles toward Europe with the incursion into the Ukraine and threats to other countries. Russia is now the largest country in the world and the second most powerful nation in the world behind the United States, according to a 2017 *US News and World Report* study.

Iran

With the discovery of oil in Iran in 1908, the Russians, Turks, and English each wanted a piece of that country. The young Shah of Iran, Ahmad Qajar, was unable to utilize Iran's new resources or withstand the intrusions, so he was overthrown by Reza Kahn of the Pahlavi dynasty, who turned the country into a constitutional monarchy in 1925. The Pahlavi dynasty governed Iran until the Islamic Revolution of 1979 orchestrated by Ayatollah Khomeini. Since 1979, Iran has rebranded itself as a force to be reckoned with and as one of only four "state sponsors of terrorism" (as defined by the US Department of State). Iran is now the 14th most powerful nation in the world (2017 *US News and World Report* study), partially due to the fact that they control 9 percent of the world's oil reserves. With Iran's recent expansion of their nuclear weapons program, the Western powers reached an agreement with them that would delay their nuclear weapons program for ten years. When this Joint Comprehensive Plan of Action was signed in 2015, Iran received $150 million dollars in sanctions relief. They also received $1.7 billion held by the United States, most of which Iran admitted would be used for their political (terrorist) agenda.

Iran has made its objectives clear: to wipe Israel, the "Little Satan," off the face of the earth, to destroy the "Great Satan," the United States, and to take over the two most holy Islamic cities of Mecca and Medina in Saudi Arabia. In an effort to accomplish these plans, they are building relationships in Iraq, Syria, and Lebanon, which will give them military access all the way to the Mediterranean. They are sponsoring Hamas terrorists in the Gaza Strip to fight Israel and insurgents in Yemen to infiltrate Saudi Arabia. Most interesting, however, is their coalition with Russia in many of these efforts.

Turkey

The country of Turkey emerged from World War I as the only territory remaining from the Ottoman Turkish Empire. They became a secular non-Islamic state and dissolved the Caliphate (Islamic leadership) in 1924. While Turkey tried to remain neutral in World War II, it entered the war in the final few months on the side of the Allies against Germany and Japan. Turkey aligned itself with Western powers when it joined NATO in 1952 and has since attempted to join the

European Union, without success. Until recent years, Turkey was the second greatest world ally to Israel, behind the United States. That has now changed.

Over the past twenty-five years, Turkey and Russia have become each other's largest trade partners, with Russia supplying most of Turkey's energy and military needs and Turkish companies operating in Russia. Turkey and Russia have developed increasingly close economic, cultural, military, and political ties. While their relationship with Russia has become strained over the Syrian conflict, they continue to work closely together on most other issues.

Turkey has become a more powerful entity in the Middle East under the leadership of Recep Erdogan, first as prime minister in 2003 and then as president since 2014. With the approval of a national referendum in April 2017, the president now has greater governmental latitude over the Parliament. President Erdogan is gradually moving Turkey from a republic to a more radical Islamist regime.

Sudan

Ezekiel 38:5 lists Ethiopia as one of the five nations in the Gog and Magog War. Today, that ancient land of Ethiopia encompasses the territory of Sudan, which is directly south of Egypt in Africa. North Sudan is another country listed by the US Department of State as one of four "state sponsors of terrorism." Their greatest political ally is Russia, which serves as its strongest investment partner and the major weapons supplier for the country.

Libya

The final nation mentioned in the Gog and Magog war of Ezekiel 38 and 39 is Libya, which is another hotbed for Islamic terrorism. Under Libyan Dictator Muammar Gaddafi, Libya and Russia were strategic military partners. In 2010 alone,

Russian arms contracts with Libya totaled 12 percent of the Kremlin's arms exports. With Libya being the largest oil producer in Africa, Russia has invested hundreds of millions of dollars in oil and gas exploration in Libya. All that changed when Gaddafi was ousted and killed in 2011. In an effort to maintain its interests in Libya, Russia is providing security forces and armament to military commander Khalifa Haftar in his bid for control of the country. Russia is gaining military and political strength with the new regime in Libya as they have been doing in Syria.

All five of these countries referenced in Ezekiel 38 as joining forces in the Gog and Magog War against Israel are currently in alliance today, with enough power to fight Israel. Russian President Vladimir Putin brought the major leaders of this coalition together on November 22, 2017 when he hosted the Turkish and Iranian leaders in Sochi to discuss the Syrian war. At no other time in history have these nations been aligned together.

The timing of the Ezekiel 38–39 prophecy will occur when Israel has returned to its land which has been "restored from the sword, whose inhabitants have been gather from many nations to the mountains of Israel which had been a continual waste; but its people were brought out from the nations, and they are living securely, all of them" (Ezekiel 38:8). These prophecies have been fulfilled, as discussed in earlier prophesies, which means the Gog and Magog War could happen at any time.

When the five nations war against Israel, it will be "to capture spoil and to seize plunder, to turn your hand against the waste places which are now inhabited, and against the people who are gathered from the nations, who have acquired cattle and goods, who live at the center of the world" (Ezekiel 38:12). Until recently, Israel had no spoil or direct assets that another nation would want. Former Israeli Prime Minister Golda Meir once quipped, "Moses took us forty years through the desert to bring us to the one spot in the Middle East that has no oil."

All that changed in 2009 and 2010 with the discovery of 22 trillion cubic feet of natural gas in the Tamar and Leviathan natural gas fields off the coast of Haifa, Israel, valued at $5 to $6 billion. The Tamar field now provides 60 percent of Israel's energy needs, with the Leviathan field allowing Israel to achieve almost total energy independence when it opens in 2019. Israel has signed an agreement with Cyprus, Greece, and Italy to construct an underwater pipeline to bring Israel's natural gas into the European market. The deal was supported by EU's Climate and Energy Commission, which said the natural gas would help limit Europe's reliance on Russian-supplied gas.

Oil and gas are Russia's most important assets. In 2012 the Russian oil-and-gas sector accounted for 16 percent of their GDP, 52 percent of Russia's federal budget revenues and over 70 percent of total exports. Experts believe the major reasons for Russia's incursion into the Ukraine in 2014 were to control their oil supply and to gain their strategic location for the exportation of that oil. Why? Because Europe needs Russia's oil! A Cambridge Econometrics Study on Oil Dependency in the EU, published in July 2016, showed that Europe has an 88 percent dependence on foreign oil. In 2015, 30 percent of its oil came Russia. Do you think it is a coincidence that Russia is supporting oil-rich countries like Iran, Syria, Libya, and Sudan?

International affairs have never played a more important role for Bible students. Now, for the first time since Ezekiel proclaimed his Gog and Magog prophecy, the world is seeing this prophecy come to life.

Prophecy 21

THE NATIONS WILL BE JUDGED FOR DIVIDING THE LAND OF ISRAEL

> For behold, in those days and at that time, when I restore the fortunes of Judah and Jerusalem, I will gather all the nations and bring them down to the valley of Jehoshaphat. Then I will enter into judgment with them there on behalf of My people and My inheritance, Israel, whom they have scattered among the nations; and they have divided up My land. (Joel 3:1–2)

While Hollywood is obsessed with apocalyptic movies, there is one aspect of their doom and gloom that is always left out: God's judgment. The Bible tells us that the nations will be judged at the time of Christ's return. One reason for that judgment is dividing up God's land—Israel.

Israel is God's land, promised as an inheritance to God's Jewish people in Genesis 12:7. He explained the size of the land in Genesis 15:8 as being "from the river of Egypt as far as the great river, the river Euphrates." King David and King Solomon conquered territories to achieve or nearly achieve those boundaries. However, their descendants gradually lost control of sections of the land until the Babylonians conquered the rest in 586 BC. From that time until the modern era, the Jewish people did not have control over their own land. That changed after World War I.

As outlined in Prophecy 7, when the Ottoman Turkish Empire was dissolved after World War I, England promised the Jews the land of their ancestors as their national homeland in a document known as the Balfour Declaration signed on November 2, 1917 (Chart 3). The Arabs subsequently agreed with that in their peace agreement with the Jews in 1919. Shortly thereafter, the land promised to the Jews was divided.

The first land division occurred in 1922 when Great Britain transferred 77 percent of the land promised to Israel to the Hashemite Kingdom known as Transjordan (Chart 4). The Peal Commission of 1936 further carved up the remaining land promised to the Jews into three sections, which amounted to only 4 percent of the original land promised to Israel (Chart 5).

Even though the Jews continued to lose landmass following each potential peace agreement, they accepted every proposal for land, but the Arabs refused every proposal.

On November 29, 1947, UN Resolution 181 proposed the final boundaries for a Jewish state and a Palestinian state, which were to take effect on May 15, 1948. The Jewish state would receive 55 percent of the remaining land, with over 60 percent of it being arid Negev desert (Chart 6). Israel accepted the boundaries; the Arabs did not.

Five Arab nations went to war against Israel on May 15, 1948. When a ceasefire ended the War of Independence fifteen months later, Israel had gained 6,000 more square miles than they had been allotted by UN Resolution 181 (Chart 7). The Arabs made their agenda known in 1949 through Azzam Pasha, then Secretary of the League of Arab States, when he said, "We have a secret weapon… and this is time. As long as we do not make peace with the Zionists, the war is not over; and as long as the war is not over, there is neither victor nor vanquished."

On August 31, 1955, Egypt's President Gamal Abdel Nasser announced, "Egypt has decided to dispatch her heroes, the disciples of Pharaoh and the sons of Islam and they will cleanse the land of Palestine.... There will be no peace on Israel's border because we demand vengeance, and vengeance is Israel's death." Over the next year, Nasser trained his "disciples of Pharaoh and sons of Islam" to engage in hostile action on the borders with Israel and to infiltrate Israel with violent acts of sabotage and murder. In addition to these acts, Nasser prevented Israel from shipping through the Suez Canal and blockaded the Gulf of Aqaba to Israeli shipping. With the backing of Britain and France, Israel responded on October 29, 1956 by capturing the Gaza Strip and the Sinai Peninsula. Israel withdrew from these newly acquired lands six months later after Egypt opened the shipping lanes (Chart 8).

In 1967, four Arab nations again fought Israel for control of the land. When the truce came after six days, Israel controlled all of its original land plus the land known to the Jews as Judea/Samaria, the Gaza Strip, the Golan Heights, and the Sinai Peninsula (Chart 9). An outcome of the Six-Day War was UN Resolution 242 that called for a "just and lasting peace" in the Middle East. For that to happen, Israel would withdraw from some territories it acquired in the war and would agree to discuss the right of return of Palestinian refugees. The Arab states would agree to peace with Israel, recognize Israel's right to exist, and negotiate toward secure borders. Israel agreed to the terms of Resolution 242. The Arabs did not and blatantly declared at their meeting in Khartoum later that year, "No peace with Israel, no recognition of Israel, no negotiations with it."

One final attempt by Israel's enemies to conquer and destroy the nation of Israel occurred in 1973 on Yom Kippur, the holiest day of the year for the Jews. After a surprise enemy attack, Israel struggled for two weeks to keep their territory. In the third week, Israel took the upper hand, fended off the assaults on all their land, and marched all the way to the outskirts of Damascus, Syria, and Cairo, Egypt.

Israel should have sovereignty over the lands they conquered during wars perpetrated on them. However, Israel returned the

Sinai Peninsula to Egypt as a result of the 1979 Peace Agreement signed between Israel and Egypt at Camp David. Israel has worked with the Palestinians in attempts to sign peace agreements that would provide land for peace. World leaders continue to coerce Israel and the Palestinians in hopes of bringing peace to the region through a two-state solution in the land of Israel.

God promises that when He returns, He will bring judgment on those nations who divide Israel. However, according to a book by Bill Koenig entitled *Eye to Eye: Facing the Consequences of Dividing Israel*, many nations who apply pressure on Israel or hold "land for peace" meetings are experiencing consequences now. One disaster occurred after President George H. W. Bush signed the Oslo Accords October 30, 1991, setting the stage for the ill-fated two-state solution. The next day, a hurricane dubbed "The Perfect Storm" traveled 1000 miles in the wrong direction and sent thirty-five-foot waves, slamming into and destroying President Bush's home in Kennebunkport, Maine.

His son, President George W. Bush worked closely with Israeli Prime Minister Ariel Sharon in giving away the Gaza Strip to the Palestinians in the first step of their statehood. When the very last Jews were dragged out of the Gaza Strip on August 23, 2005, a tropical depression in the Atlantic Ocean turned into Hurricane Katrina and made landfall in New Orleans days later. It was the deadliest hurricane in US history, with 2,000 people dead and property damage exceeding $81 billion. Are these coincidences, or was God showing His displeasure for dividing His land?

Ever since 1922, nations have tried to chop the land rightfully belonging to the Jews into little pieces. This will continue until Jesus Christ returns and brings judgment against these nations for dividing His land, as promised in Joel 3:2. This prophecy could not be fulfilled at any time over the past 2500 years until now with Israel restored as a nation and in control of their ancestral land.

Prophecy 22

THE WHOLE WORLD WILL GATHER AGAINST JERUSALEM

Behold, I am going to make Jerusalem a cup that causes reeling to all the peoples around; and when the siege is against Jerusalem, it will also be against Judah. It will come about in that day that I will make Jerusalem a heavy stone for all the peoples; all who lift it will be severely injured. And all the nations of the earth will be gathered against it. (Zechariah 12:3)

O y Vey! Here they come again! Individual nations have fought for control of Jerusalem for centuries. However, this prophecy written in about 520 BC predicts an end times siege when *all* (emphasis mine) the nations will gather against God's holy city. How is it possible for all nations to fight at the same time in one location? There is an answer that has only been possible during the past seventy-plus years.

After experiencing the horrors of World War I, the nations organized an international body designed to prevent war and to promote world peace. The League of Nations was formed in 1920 representing sixty-three nations before its demise as a result of World War II.

The United Nations replaced the League of Nations in 1945. Its main purposes are to maintain worldwide peace and security, develop relations among nations, and foster cooperation between nations in order to solve economic, social, cultural, or humanitarian international problems.

According to most sources, there are 195 countries in the world today. Of these, 193 are members of the United Nations, and two (Palestine and The Vatican) are non-member observer states. Therefore, the United Nations represents the entire world as it carries out its objectives.

As evidenced by ongoing wars and world hostilities, the United Nations has proven ineffective in maintaining peace and fostering cooperation among member nations. By their own actions, they have adopted an unofficial bias against Israel while ignoring other conflicts throughout the world.

- From 1955 to 2013, the UN Security Council passed seventy-seven resolutions against Israel and only one against Palestine.
- Between 2012 and 2015, the UN General Assembly adopted ninety-seven resolutions criticizing countries, with eighty-three of them being against Israel (86%).
- In 2013, the UN General Assembly adopted twenty-one resolutions criticizing Israel but only four resolutions condemning other nations (Syria, Iran, North Korea, and Myanmar).
- From the creation of the UN Human Rights Council in 2006, it has adopted 135 resolutions criticizing countries, sixty-eight of which (over 50%) were against Israel.
- Each year, the World Health Organization (WHO) meets to address global health issues. They have singled out only one country to condemn: Israel.
- The International Labour Organization (ILO) was established to improve conditions of labor, work hours, unemployment, wages, and so forth. At its annual

conference in 2014, the ILO produced only one country-specific report that castigated Israel.

• In 2014, there were over 750 violent anti-Semitic acts worldwide, which was an increase of 38 percent from 2013. The UN took no action to condemn these anti-Semitic acts or the people who performed them.

According to their website, the United Nations has "over 90,000 military personnel contributed by national armies from across the globe." In addition, Articles 52 to 54 of the UN Charter permit nations to form "regional arrangements" for the purpose of maintaining "international peace and security." The 1949 North Atlantic Treaty Organization (NATO) was the first such "arrangement."

NATO and other "regional arrangements" are not allowed to undertake any action "without the authorization of the [UN] Security Council." Furthermore, Article 54 requires "regional arrangements" to report their contemplative plans and all activities to the UN Security Council. Clearly the United Nations, which represents all the nations of the earth, has armies at its disposal to do their bidding, including members of the US armed forces.

US forces have carried out UN missions during recent decades. President George H. W. Bush cited authorization from a UN Security Council resolution in 1992 to send 30,000 US troops into Somalia. Under Bill Clinton's presidency in April 1994, a British UN troop commander, paired with a UN diplomat from Japan, gave the order for US fighter planes from NATO to attack targets in Bosnia. President Clinton sent tens of thousands of American troops to Haiti in September 1994 to enforce another UN resolution. In March 2011, President Obama deployed US forces in the NATO air war against Libya that was authorized by a UN Security Council resolution.

In 1994, US Army Specialist Michael G. New was to be dispatched to the command of the UN in Macedonia. As such, he was ordered to wear the arm patch and hat designating him a soldier of the United Nations. New objected to changing his allegiance to the United Nations from the US Constitution, which he promised in an oath to defend. He was later charged and given a bad conduct discharge from the army.

The UN has developed into a powerful entity representing the entire world. The UN periodically sends different armies of the world to uphold its resolutions. Since most of its resolutions are against Israel, could the UN be the catalyst to represent all the nations of the world in the upcoming battle against Jerusalem? That possibility never existed before 1945, yet it exists today.

Part Two:

GENERAL PROPHECIES

Prophecy 23

FALSE PROPHETS

> And Jesus answered and said to them, "See to it
> that no one misleads you. For many will come
> in My name, saying, 'I am the Christ,' and will
> mislead many... Many false prophets will arise
> and will mislead many... For false Christs and
> false prophets will arise and will show great
> signs and wonders, so as to mislead, if possible,
> even the elect." (Matthew 24:4, 11, 24)

In Matthew 24, Jesus' disciples asked Him, "When will these
things happen (destruction of the temple), and what will
be the sign of Your coming, and of the end of the age?" Jesus
spent the rest of the chapter answering the last two questions
regarding what signs to be looking for in preparation for His
return. The next several prophesies will focus on nine of the
signs Jesus mentioned.

Jesus' first and greatest warning sign of what to look for
before He returns is false prophets and false messiahs who will
come in His name. This is so important that Jesus mentions the
same problem in at least six different verses in Matthew 24.
He expresses grave concern that these false leaders will be so
persuasive that they might be able to lead even the elect astray.

False messiahs have been prevalent in every generation.
Wikipedia lists sixty-two false messiahs since the time of

Christ, not including the plethora of religious cults that have developed. What then makes these days different so as to fulfill Jesus' prophecies?

In recent decades, with the rise of TV, the Internet, and social media, there has been a new platform for hearing and seeing charismatic leaders full of "enlightened" understanding that lead people astray. Many individuals or their followers have claimed the messianic title including infamous people like Jim Jones of Jonestown, Sun Myung Moon of the Unification Church, Rabbi Menachem Schneerson founder of the Chabad Lubavitch Movement, David Koresh of the Branch Davidians, and lesser known "messiahs" like Miami's José Luis de Jesús Miranda of the Creciendo en Gracia sect, Brazilian Alvara Theiss from Suprema Ordem Universal da Santissima Trindade, Russian Sergey Anatolyevitch Torop of the Church of the Last Testament, and Judith Zebra Knight channeling at the Ramtha School of Enlightenment in Washington. The list continues to grow larger as more individuals emerge and state that only they know and speak the truth.

Any group which claims to be Christian but does not adhere to biblical truth would be considered a cult. Any leader or group which uses psychological techniques to recruit and manipulate its members would also be labeled a cult. There are thousands of organizations worldwide that fit that category. In France alone, thirty groups were branded cults by the National Assembly of France in 1995. The International Church of Cannabis opened in Denver, Colorado, in 2016 with a membership list of 1400 people. The Church of Satan started in San Francisco, California, in 1966 and now has an active international presence. The list is endless of leaders and organizations that adhere to false teaching.

Probably the most infamous false Christ is the Islamic distortion of the true Jesus Christ of the Bible. Muslims acknowledge some truths of the historical Jesus, such as His virgin birth, His being a prophet, His teachings on love, His miracles, and His return to earth. But, they categorically reject the gospel message that is the foundation of the Christian faith. They deny that Jesus is God, that He died to save mankind from their sins, and that He rose from the dead. When anyone says they believe in Jesus, it's important to investigate that statement further to see if they believe in the true Lord Jesus Christ of the Bible or one of their own making.

According to many books, Muslims believe their Jesus, called Isa, will return to earth, be a just ruler, believe in and instruct others on the Quran and Hadith (Muslim teachings and traditions), submit himself to the 12th Imam, lead the people in Muslim prayer and live on earth for forty years during a time of peace and prosperity. The bottom line of the Muslim prophetic beliefs is that Jesus will not return as King of kings and Lord of lords as the Bible says, but will come instead denouncing Christianity and humbly submitting to the Muslim Allah, the 12th Imam, Islam, and the Quran. He will reject all aspects of Christianity, tear down Christian crosses and tell all his followers to do the same. These false beliefs and this false Isa may well be the final false Christ to wreak havoc on a biblically uneducated, gullible, and spiritually immature society.

Jesus' warnings of false prophets and false Christs could be directed toward the Jewish people since the text of Matthew 24 includes many Jewish references. If so, the Jews will have to be watchful so as not to be fooled by someone appearing to be their long-awaited messiah. According to Judaism 101 from *http:// www.jewfaq.org/mashiach.htm*, the Jews are looking for their messiah who "will be a charismatic leader, inspiring others to follow his example. He will be a great military leader, who will win battles for Israel. He will be a great judge, who makes righteous decisions." That description better matches the Antichrist than the biblical Messiah. The Jews could be easily distracted from the truth by a man who matches their criteria and expectations of the Messiah.

The world is seeing more "signs and wonders" in our generation than any other since the time of Christ. Some of these signs have been considered genuine miracles. Jesus has been revealing Himself to people visibly and in dreams throughout Third World countries and protecting them through impossible circumstances. Because of that, many Muslims and Jews have converted to Christianity, and that is the ultimate purpose of God's miracles. But, where the truth is, there will always be a counterfeit. That is why John commanded us to test the spirits to see whether they are from God (1 John 4:1–3). After all, there is nothing quite like a good miracle to focus people on the miraculous rather than on God.

Consider the phenomena at Medjugorje in Bosnia and Herzegovina where the Virgin Mary began appearing to six children. These individuals, now adults, continue to experience this apparition annually on June 24. In these apparitions, as in others at Fatima, Lourdes, and Guadalupe, a lady-like figure, who is identified as the Virgin Mary, appears and speaks spiritual words to the children. In reading a book about Medjugorje, I found that 90 percent of the words attributed to the Virgin Mary matched with scriptural truths. However, the other 10 percent do not, and, actually go against biblical truths. Nothing that is of God or from God will ever contradict the word of God. As a result of the miraculous appearances at Medjugorje and other places, millions are worshipping Mary, who is the object of the miracles, rather than Jesus, the Author and Perfecter of our faith. Satan twists the truth and manipulates with half-truths to draw people into his bidding and away from God (just look at the story of Adam and Eve in Genesis 3).

One might think that since a miracle is mostly accurate, it must be from God. But, a friend once told me, "Satan will agree with you nine times, so you will agree with him the tenth!" Jesus' brother explained that better in James 2:10, "For whoever keeps the whole law and yet stumbles in one point, he has become guilty of all." The Catholic Church has not officially confirmed these miracles, though they continue to encourage people to make pilgrimages to the sites. It is reported that over 30 million Catholics have visited Medjugorje in the past thirty-six years.

It is easy to understand how people can be led astray from the truth. In this day and age, few people read and study the Bible. According to a Barna survey in 2009, only 9 percent of adult Americans hold a biblical worldview. Many people are gleaning their "spiritual" knowledge from such Hollywood movies as *Noah*, *Moses*, and *The Shack* and leave with misperceptions of truth. Writers on the Internet provide so many different interpretations of the same biblical passage that the most eager students can be confused. As our culture changes, people think that the Bible should change with it and should be reinterpreted based on modern beliefs or actions. That leads to biblical misinterpretation and disagreements based on opinion rather than on truth.

People generally rely on their own feelings, desires, or backgrounds to determine what truth is, picking and choosing what they want to believe. Once they have reinterpreted the truth, they look for others who hold like-minded views. The Bible explains, "For the time will come when they will not endure sound doctrine; but wanting to have their ears tickled, they will accumulate for themselves teachers in accordance to their own desires" (2 Timothy 4:3). Sliding down the slippery slope from truth opens the door to believe false teaching and a different gospel.

Jesus refers to deceivers in the last days as "false Christs" who may regard themselves as genuine believers in Christ and may be actively working for Him. They could even be our pastors and church leaders.

For two years, researcher George Barna contacted pastors around the country to determine their beliefs about Scripture, moral and political issues, and the content of their sermons in light of their beliefs. The conclusions he shared in 2014 were that 90 percent of the pastors surveyed believe the Bible speaks to moral and political issues, but only 10 percent of them are preaching on the issues. That means only a small portion of church members is hearing biblical sermons relevant to the important situations shaping our world. How can people live by the Bible if they are not learning truths from the Bible?

In addition, when these pastors were asked how they gauge the success of their churches, they generally listed five factors: attendance, giving, number of programs, number of staff, and square footage of church. My response would have focused on transformed lives, salvations, baptisms, mission work, and so forth. After all, the purpose of the church is not to build itself up but to guide others as believers and disciples of Jesus Christ.

Some of these church leaders may even be prophesying in the name of Jesus and working miracles in His name. But, if they are not following the true Jesus Christ of the Bible and all His teachings, they are serving a false Christ. "Many will say to Me on that day, 'Lord, Lord, did we not prophesy in Your name, and in Your name cast out demons, and in Your name perform many miracles?' And then I will declare to them, 'I never knew you; depart from Me, you who practice lawlessness'" (Matthew 7:22, 23).

Many new detrimental movements have surfaced within the Christian churches these past several decades such as the emergent church, Chrislam, and progressive Christianity. According to Wikipedia, progressive Christianity "seeks to reform the faith via the insights of post-modernism and a reclaiming of the truth beyond the verifiable historicity and factuality of the passages in the Bible.... It developed out of the liberal Christianity of the modern-era, which was rooted in enlightenment thinking." In order words, progressive Christianity is interpreting the Bible based on culture rather than on truth.

One group of progressive Christian leaders recruited 160 pastors from mainline Christian denominations in Arizona to sign the Phoenix Declaration document in 2002. They see this document as the theological backbone for progressive Christianity in the United States. While there are several aspects to their approved statement, such as a strong support for the LGBTQX community within the Christian hierarchy and churches, their first point is a belief that there are many ways to

God. They state in their study guide that, "Christian love of God includes walking fully in the path of Jesus, without denying the legitimacy of other paths God may provide humanity." They focus on Jesus' call to love and to help humanity while ignoring Jesus' message that, "I [Jesus] am the way, and the truth, and the life; no one comes to the Father but through Me" (John 14:6). The apostle Paul explains the foundation for these defectors in 2 Corinthians 11:13–15 when he writes:

> For such men are false apostles, deceitful workers, disguising themselves as apostles of Christ. No wonder, for even Satan disguises himself as an angel of light. Therefore it is not surprising if his servants also disguise themselves as servants of righteousness, whose end will be according to their deeds.

Unfortunately, it is easy for people to be led astray by charismatic speakers who manipulate with their smooth-sounding speech and potentially miraculous works. They throw out hope or false assurance, exalting those who follow as the chosen or "enlightened" people. According to Revelation 13, the Antichrist will do these exact things to cause people to worship him. After all, Satan is alive and well on Planet Earth, and he is no dummy! He doesn't come to us in a red suit, with a pitchfork and goatee. Instead, he disguises himself as an angel of light, so he can manipulate us away from God without our realizing it. The only weapon against false leaders and false teaching is the truth: "and you will know the truth, and the truth will make you free" (John 8:32).

Prophecy 24

WARS AND RUMORS OF WARS

You will be hearing of wars and rumors of wars. See that you are not frightened, for those things must take place, but that is not yet the end. For nation will rise against nation, and kingdom against kingdom... But all these things are merely the beginning of birth pangs. (Matthew 24:6-8)

The July 6, 2003 *New York Times* article, "What Every Person Should Know About War," claimed that over the past 3,400 years, humans have only experienced peace 8 percent of the time (268 years of peace). America has a similar record, enjoying peace for only 8 percent of our history (19 of 241 years in peace). With the wars experienced throughout most of human history, how will we recognize the wars that Jesus says will be prevalent in these last days?

The timing of the prophecy in Matthew 24 is associated with birth pangs. Any woman who has experienced childbirth knows that birth pangs are a painful and progressive prelude to the birth. They grow in frequency and intensity until the labor pangs take over, and the child is eventually born. Jesus uses this example to indicate that wars and other catastrophes will escalate until the final seven years of labor, which we know to be the Tribulation. Jesus describes the labor of the Tribulation as "such as has not occurred since the beginning of the world until now, nor ever shall" (Matthew 24:21).

Some prophecy scholars believe that the phrase "nation will rise against nation and kingdom against kingdom" refers to the two "wars to end all wars," meaning World War I and World War II. That prophecy could also point to the increase of wars and their severity in these last several decades through the many civil wars, Middle East infighting, African territorial battles, ISIL, Russian incursions, China South Sea disputes, revolutions, and warnings of annihilation by terrorist countries like Iran and North Korea. As a matter of fact, of the 195 nations in the world, only ten of them were considered free of conflict in 2016 (Global Peace Index).

More people died from wars in the 20th century than in all the previous generations in human history. Certainly the lethal condition of the modern world matches with the birth pangs of war. However, Jesus may well have been referring to something different.

In the Olivet Discourse in Matthew 24, Jesus is speaking to his Jewish disciples about the Jewish temple and using many phrases that are uniquely Jewish, such as "abomination of desolation," "Daniel the prophet," and "Sabbath." Could Jesus' warning about the wars be referring to wars the Jewish nation will experience in the last days? If so, He would be referencing wars that the nation of Israel would experience in the last days. Since Israel has only been a nation since 1948, these wars would deal with situations experienced in Israel since then.

Prophecy 17 details the more than a dozen wars Israel has experienced in the past seventy years. In addition, Palestinians have perpetrated thousands of suicide bombings, stabbings, terror attacks, rocket firings, and riots on Jewish citizens since the nation's founding. The terrorist organizations of Hezbollah in Lebanon and Hamas in the Gaza Strip have dug hundreds of tunnels to infiltrate Jewish cities and kill Israeli civilians. They have stockpiled nearly 200,000 rockets on Israel's borders with the promise to use them. Iran has threatened to wipe Israel off the face of the earth. Threat of war is always on the horizon in Israel. All Jewish citizens are to be on alert at all times for any uprising or war. Clearly, Israel is constantly hearing about and living through the fear of "wars and rumors of wars."

Even with the constant threat of wars, Israel is one of the safest places in the world to visit. The Palestinians threaten the Israelis in their everyday environment, not the tourists at tourist sites. Israel's national security and local police respond immediately to any threats or acts of violence.

Keep in mind, there are still several battles and wars to take place before Jesus returns, as have been outlined in other prophesies. Keep praying for Israel as they continue to endure threats of war.

Prophecy 25

FAMINES

And in various places there will be famines and
earthquakes. But all these things are merely the
beginning of birth pangs. (Matthew 24:7b, 8)

W e have all been horrified by images of the results of
starvation, bloated children with skin clinging tightly,
outlining every bone in their bodies. It seems unimaginable that
in this modern era, people around the world would suffer from
lack of food. It is not only happening, but it is getting worse.

Famines are caused by varying combinations of economic
backwardness, poor governance, dictators, drought, frost, pestilence, natural disasters, and war. They are nothing new as
the first one in Scripture dates back to the time of Abraham in
Genesis 12:10. Yet, Jesus mentions famines as one of the signs
pointing to the time period before His return.

In the past century, the world has experienced the worst
famines in all of human history. Some have been caused by
ruthless governments like the Soviet Union whose genocide
resulted in the deaths of up to 10 million people in the Ukraine
and about 6 million Soviet citizens from 1932 to 1933. Mao
Zedong orchestrated China's "Great Leap Forward" famine
from 1958 to 1962 that killed some 15 million people. Overall,
cruel dictators were responsible for the deaths of over 70 million people from starvation between 1920 and 1962.

Much of world hunger and famine is a result of war which destroys the land and the crops. With all the wars discussed in the previous prophesies that have and will continue to occur, it is no wonder famines have increased at epidemic proportions. Revelation 6:5–6 provides biblical evidence that famine follows war.

It goes without saying that famine increases proportionately with population growth. The world population in December 2017 was 7.6 billion people (Wikipedia). The United Nations expects that number to increase to between 11.2 billion and 16 billion by the year 2100.

One of the most important global warming programs of the United Nations is known as "sustainable development." In 2015, the United Nations adopted seventeen goals designed to end hunger and poverty, protect the planet, and ensure prosperity for all. These goals will be met through a redistribution of wealth and resources from developing countries to underdeveloped countries. While the goal to end hunger and poverty is a laudable one, Jesus says that will never happen. Instead, the problem will continue to intensify until Jesus returns.

There is much controversy and conflicting reports regarding global warming. If it impacts our world as some report, there will be water and agricultural scarcity. A 2013 study by Dr. Jacob Schewe of the Potsdam Institute for Climate Impact Research found "the combination of unmitigated climate change and further population growth will expose a significant fraction of the world population" (15 percent of the global population) to "chronic or absolute water scarcity" (by another 40 percent)." In other words, population growth will cause further water scarcity in the world.

Water scarcity in turn will have a dramatic impact on agriculture. A study by the Proceedings for the National Academy of Sciences (PNAS) of current agricultural models estimates that climate change will directly reduce food production from maize, soybeans, wheat, and rice by as much as 43 percent by the end of the 21st century.

Wikipedia reports forty-five famines in the past one hundred years, more than in any century in history. The World Health Organization states that one-third of the world is well fed, one-third is underfed, and one-third is starving. Statistics show that between 9 and 15 million people die each year from starvation.

Arif Husain, UN World Food Program Chief Economist, told Reuters in a February 2017 interview that 20 million people would starve in the next six months due to four separate famines. "In my not quite 15 years with the World Food Programme, this is the first time that we are literally talking about famine in four different parts of the world (Yemen, South Sudan, Somalia, Nigeria) at the same time," he told Reuters.

As in the previous prophecy, these end times famines are compared with birth pangs, meaning they will occur more often and increase in intensity until the return of Jesus Christ. Based on modern history and scientific predictions, this prophecy is progressing as foretold.

Prophecy 26

EARTHQUAKES

> And in various places there will be famines and
> earthquakes. But all these things are merely the
> beginning of birth pangs. (Matthew 24:7b, 8)

" Shake, Rattle and Roll" was recorded by Bill Haley and His Comets in 1960. Little did they know the world would continue to "shake, rattle and roll" until Jesus returns. Jesus lays out another prophecy that will escalate in the final days before His return. This prophecy of earthquakes, like the prophecies before it, is compared to birth pangs that increase in frequency and intensity before the final labor pains arrive. This means the world will experience more quakes that are stronger than at previous times in history.

An earthquake is a trembling or shaking movement of the Earth's surface resulting from the shifting of the earth's tectonic plates. Those closest to the fault lines experience the worst effects. Hundreds of earthquakes occur worldwide every day, but most of them are so small they can only be detected on the Richter scale.

The Richter scale was developed in 1935 to measure the magnitude of the earth's movement. It followed the Mercalli intensity scale of the late 1800s that detected more the effects of earthquakes than the energy from them. In the 1970s, the Moment Magnitude Scale became the instrument used by the

US Geological Survey to measure the energy released from quakes, though the Richter scale is the more common term used to describe the intensity of quakes. Have earthquakes really increased or is it just the perception due to better monitoring and technology?

About 350 earthquake-monitoring stations operated in the world in 1931. There are now more than 4,000 stations providing second-by-second detailed earthquake reporting. The technology and timely receipt of data identifies more and smaller earthquakes that had previously gone undetected. Are these previously undetected earthquakes the increase in earthquakes that Jesus was talking about? I doubt it since few people even know they have occurred.

Since 1900, there have been more than 10,000 strong earthquakes with magnitudes of 6 or greater around the world, according to the US Geological Survey. Energy, Mines and Resources Canada reported in the early 1990s that between 1900 and 1969 there were an average of six earthquakes per decade, registering 6.5 or more on the Richter scale. In the following two decades, that number increased to thirty-three earthquakes, measuring at least 6.5 per decade. In the first two years of the 1990s, that number had skyrocketed to an average of six hundred earthquakes per decade, averaging 6.5 or more.

Of the twenty most powerful earthquakes recorded in history, fifteen have occurred since 1946, with three of them recorded in the past ten years. The US Geological Survey website states:

> Within the central and eastern United States, the number of earthquakes has increased dramatically over the past few years. Between the years 1973–2008, there was an average of 21 earthquakes of magnitude three and larger in the central and eastern United States. This rate has ballooned to over 600 M3+ (magnitude 3 or higher) earthquakes in 2014 and over 1000

in 2015. Through August 2016, over 500 M3+ earthquakes have occurred in 2016.

In 2015 alone, Oklahoma experienced an unprecedented 907 earthquakes ranked 3.0 or higher on the Richter scale. The rate of earthquake occurrences in that state has increased 4000 percent in the past eight years. Their neighbor, Texas, has experienced a six-fold increase in earthquake rates in the last decade. Most people believe the increases in these two states are manmade due to oil fracking. But, they are earthquakes nonetheless.

With the noted increase in the number and intensity of earthquakes, geologists insist this is simply a periodic phenomenon. In the *Geophysical Research Letters*, author Tom Parsons, a research geophysicist with the US Geological Survey in Menlo Park, California, stated that even though the global earthquake rate is on the rise, the number of quakes could still be explained by random chance. Other geologists insist that earthquake numbers increase and decrease consistently, so it would be inaccurate to state that earthquakes are on the rise, even though evidence strongly suggests they are.

The Bible mentions or alludes to earthquakes nearly twenty times. Earthquakes are generally mentioned as drawing people closer to God (1 Kings 19:11; Matthew 27:24) or pronouncing judgment (Isaiah 29:6; Numbers 16:32). Perhaps the earthquakes Jesus is referring to in Matthew 24 could be God's way of pouring out His mercy to draw people to Himself before it's too late—before the catastrophic earthquakes explained in the book of Revelation occur. These Revelation quakes depict God's wrath poured out on an unbelieving world throughout the seven-year Tribulation period. They are described in the sixth seal (Revelation 6:12), seventh trumpet (Revelation 8:5; 11:13; 11:19), and the seventh bowl judgments (Revelation 16:18). These Revelation earthquakes are no longer the "birth pangs" leading to labor but will be the real and painful labor.

Prophecy 27

PESTILENCE

And there shall be famines, and pestilences, and earthquakes, in diverse places. All these are the beginning of sorrows. (Matthew 24:7b, 8, KJV)

I n the original Greek language of the New Testament, Jesus used the word *loimos* to point out that pestilence, disease, and plagues will increase and escalate worldwide as the time of His return nears. While the world has seen its share of maladies, they are nothing compared to what is happening today.

Pestilence is always equated with judgment on Israel or the nations for their disobedience. Consider the desolation caused by the plagues in Egypt as recorded in Exodus 7–11 or the locust devastation explained in Joel 1–2 or the disease of leprosy outlined in Leviticus 13–14. Deuteronomy 28:21 lists pestilence as one of the many curses equated with disobedience to God and His laws: "The Lord will make the pestilence cling to you until He has consumed you from the land where you are entering to possess it." God associates pestilence with "sword and famine" in nineteen verses in the Bible, tying all these judgments together. This would indicate that the pestilences that will intensify in these last days are a sign of God's impending judgment before and at His return.

The most infamous worldwide plague in history was the Eurasia Black Plague that killed an estimated 20 million people in Europe and perhaps 100 million worldwide, wiping out over one-third of the European population from 1347 to 1352. DNA analysis indicates that the pathogen involved several forms of plague including the bubonic plague. While the bubonic plague is not extinct, it has been curbed through modern medicine and public health practices. The current pestilences we are experiencing and will experience during the Tribulation are injuring and/or killing considerably more than the Black Plague. Scientists have identified over three hundred new diseases since 1940. Following the development of penicillin in 1942, many epidemics have been constrained while others continue to flourish and mutate. Consider the following pandemics that are ravaging our world today:

- Cancer is the leading cause of death worldwide each year. In 2015, over 90 million people had cancer, with 14 million new cases being diagnosed each year. Eight million people die from cancer per year. The National Cancer Institute projects that there will be 21 million new cancer cases each year by 2030, with a mortality rate of 13 million per year.
- The HIV virus known as AIDs first emerged in 1981. It has grown to a global pandemic, with 38.5 million people infected with the virus at the end of 2016, resulting in one million deaths each year.
- The deadly Ebola virus was first discovered in 1976 and has a mortality rate of 50 percent of those who contract the disease. While it has mostly been contained in Africa, many known cases have spread to other parts of the world.
- More than 110 million Americans have a sexually transmitted disease. It is estimated that nearly half of Americans will suffer the effects of these diseases at some point in their lifetime.
- Due to the overuse of antibiotics, a new generation of "superbugs" is arising. Staph and MRSA infections have

become rampant in hospitals due to weakened immune systems of the patients. Nearly 20,000 people die each year in the United States from drug-resistant staph infections. MRSA is resistant to most antibiotics, which is why it is sometimes called the "Super Bug." MRSA killed over 11,000 people in the United States in 2011.

- The H5N1 bird flu is considered by specialists to be the most serious pandemic threat on earth today because it mutates so quickly and easily that vaccines are obsolete before they can be effective. The World Health Organization estimates a 60 percent mortality rate if this flu becomes widespread.

- Serious but less deadly viruses such as Marburg, Enterovirus, and Chikungunya and Lassa fevers were not even on most people's radar in 2014.

- While vaccines have been developed that have nearly eradicated some diseases like smallpox, polio, measles, mumps, and tuberculosis, some of these diseases are again resurfacing around the world.

- The number of malaria cases in the African countries of Guinea, Liberia, and Sierra Leone increased by 3.5 million cases in 2016.

- Fallout from nuclear radiation will continue to cause major health problems. For example, the meltdown at the Fukushima Daiichi nuclear power plant in Japan in 2011 has caused three hundred tons of contaminated, radioactive water to leak into the Pacific Ocean every day. Cancer rates have spiked in Japan since the incident. The dangerous and radioactive isotope known as Seaborne Cesium 134 has shown up on the shores of Tillamook Bay in Oregon as detected by the Woods Hole Oceanographic Institution.

- Air pollution in China alone has been linked to 6 million deaths per year. Air pollution is even worse in the United Arab Emirates, with 80 micrograms of pollutants per cubic meter, compared to China's 73.

This is just a short list of germ-related and environmental-related concerns that have surfaced in the past several decades. Certainly with the population explosion, there will be more deaths overall from each ailment. Diseases will continue to spread more rapidly in the world due to a lack of basic medical care, the ease of worldwide travel, the migration of nearly 60 million refugees, and the mutation of germs. Link those with the desolation caused by wars and industrial pollution, and these problems will continue to escalate.

Pestilence will reach its pinnacle during the Tribulation period when a fourth of the earth will be killed "with sword and with famine and with pestilence and by the wild beasts of the earth" (Revelation 6:8). The city of Mystery Babylon will later be destroyed in one day according to Revelation 18:8 when, "her plagues will come, pestilence and mourning and famine, and she will be burned up with fire; for the Lord God who judges her is strong."

Prophecy 28

HATED BY ALL NATIONS

Then they will deliver you to tribulation, and
will kill you, and you will be hated by all nations
because of My name. (Matthew 24:9)

"Then" is a timeframe, signifying the speaker is moving
from one time period to another. In the case of Matthew
24, Jesus has finished describing the birth pangs and has now
moved on to the Tribulation period. In other words, intermittent
birth pains that increased and intensified have now gone into
full-blown labor. The labor pains will be much worse than the
birth pangs in frequency and in suffering. They will not stop
until the birth process is complete, which, in this case, represents the return of Jesus Christ. The world has yet to experience these labor pains (called the Tribulation), so statistics
are not available to show the martyrdom depicted in Jesus'
prophecy. However, data is available to prove how Jews and
Christians are currently being hated by all nations on account
of Jesus, which lays the foundation for future prejudice.

The context in Matthew 24 refers to tribulation for the
Jewish people. Could the passage represent persecution for the
followers of Jesus Christ also? Let's examine both situations
to see if they apply.

The period knows as the Tribulation in the Bible is described
by many other titles including "the time of Jacob's trouble"

(Jeremiah 30:7), the "seventieth week of Daniel" (Daniel 9:27), and the "day of their (Israel's) calamity" (Deuteronomy 32:35). The prophet Zephaniah describes the Tribulation for the Jews as, "A day of wrath is that day, a day of trouble and distress, a day of destruction and desolation, a day of darkness and gloom, a day of clouds and thick darkness" (Zephaniah 1:15). Daniel 12:1 recounts this time period pessimistically, "Now at that time Michael, the great prince who stands guard over the sons of your people, will arise. And there will be a time of distress such as never occurred since there was a nation until that time."

Why will all the nations hate the Jews and set out to kill them? As King Solomon pointed out, "there is nothing new under the sun" (Ecclesiastes 1:9). The world has hated and persecuted the Jewish people for centuries, so why would it be any different now?

Persecution of the Jewish people first began in Egypt when Pharaoh became jealous and feared that they would become "more and mightier than we [the Egyptians]" (Exodus 1:9). He subjugated them to slavery when he "appointed taskmasters over them to afflict them with hard labor. And they built for Pharaoh storage cities, Pithom and Raamses" (Exodus 1:11)."

Centuries later, the Assyrians invaded and conquered the northern kingdom of Israel in 722 BC, taking captives into exile (2 Kings 17:4–6). The southern kingdom of Judah experienced the same fate 136 years thereafter when the Babylonians conquered Jerusalem and marched captives to Babylon (2 Kings 25:8–11). In the 2nd century BC, Seleucid King Antiochus IV Epiphanes made a proclamation that all his kingdom should be one people, thus forcing the Jews to give up their own religion. When Jews did not adhere to his decree, they were put to death. Women who had their children circumcised were killed, their babies were hung around their necks, and all who participated in the circumcision were killed along with them (1 Maccabees 1 in the Apocrypha).

When Jesus came as the Jewish Messiah, the Jewish leaders manipulated the people to reject Him (John 1:11; Matthew

27:22, 23). Ever since then, many Christians blamed the Jews for killing Jesus and persecuted them for it. However, Jesus willingly gave up His life in order to redeem mankind and pay the penalty for their sins (John 10:17, 18; 3:16). Jesus told Pilate that no one had authority to kill Him unless it had been granted by the Father (John 19:11). So, instead of persecuting the Jews for 2000 years for something they did not do, we should thank them for what they did do. They gave us the Jewish Messiah to save us from the penalty of eternal death.

Because the Jewish people, in general, rejected Jesus Christ as their Messiah, many early Church fathers taught that the believing church replaced the apostate Jewish people as God's chosen people. In a writing attributed to Barnabas of Alexandria between AD 130 and 138, he stated, "Take heed to yourselves and be not like some, piling up sins and saying that the covenant is theirs as well as ours. It is ours, but they lost it completely just after Moses received it." A few years later, Justin Martyr (AD 100–165) blasted the Jews for rejecting and killing Jesus and for leading people away from salvation. His writings became incorporated into early Christian thought and were the origins of Christian anti-Semitism.

Origen of Alexandria (AD 185–254) made this point clear when he said:

> We may thus assert in utter confidence that the Jews will not return to their earlier situation, for they have committed the most abominable of crimes, in forming this conspiracy against the Savior of the human race... hence the city where Jesus suffered was necessarily destroyed, the Jewish nation was driven from its country, and another people was called by God to the blessed election.

While some popes and Christian princes stepped up to protect Jews, the Christian crusades of AD 1096 to 1270 were an anathema to the Jewish people and a black eye for Christians. The Crusaders first struck the Jewish communities of Speyer, Worms, Mainz, and Cologne in Europe. Jews were offered the option of conversion to Christianity or death. In the case of the Crusades, somewhere between 3,000 to 10,000 Jews in those cities were killed rather than give up their beliefs.

The Crusaders made their way to Jerusalem in AD 1099. Once there, they gathered all the Jews of Jerusalem into the central synagogue and set fire to it. Some Jews climbed to the top of the Al-Aksa mosque on the Temple Mount but were caught and beheaded. The Crusader leader, Godfrey of Bouillon, wrote to the Pope, "If you want to know what has been done with the enemy found in Jerusalem... our people had their vile blood up to the knees of their horses." These Crusades set a dangerous precedent—the rise of organized, popular, anti-Jewish uprisings from that point on (excerpts taken from *www.chabad.org*).

Salo Baron, described as the greatest Jewish historian of the 20th century, summed up the effects of the Crusades when he wrote:

> The trail of blood and smoldering ruins left behind in the Jewish communities from France to Palestine... for the first time brought home to the Jewish people, its foes and friends, the utter instability of the Jewish position in the western world... from the First Crusade on, anti-Jewish persecutions exercised a dangerously contagious appeal, which in periods of great emotional stress degenerated into mass psychosis transcending national boundaries.

The list of historic anti-Semitism is too long to transcribe. But a few infamous examples through the centuries include expulsion from England (1290), forced conversion or expulsion during the Spanish Inquisition (1492), condemnation by Martin Luther in writings such as *On the Jews and Their Lies*

(1543), expulsion and murder in the Russian pogroms (1881–1906), and ruthless treatment and extermination in the Nazi Holocaust during World War II.

In this modern age of tolerance, one would expect anti-Semitism to be eradicated. On the contrary, it has grown to epidemic proportions. Jews have been expelled or forced under duress to leave the twenty-two Arab nations in the past several decades. Jews who continue to live in predominately Muslim countries are subjected to enormous pressure and anti-Semitic attacks. Former Iranian President Mahmoud Ahmadinejad has consistently declared he will wipe Israel (the Jewish people) off the face of the earth. Palestinian President Mahmoud Abbas has publicly stated that no Jew will be allowed in their future state.

It is not surprising to hear those hate-filled remarks against Jews because that is the attitude Muslims learn from their religious writings. In the Islamic Hadith 6985, Muslims are told, "The last hour would not come unless the Muslims will fight against the Jews and the Muslims would kill them until the Jews would hide themselves behind a stone or a tree and a stone or a tree would say: Muslim, or the servant of Allah, there is a Jew behind me; come and kill him..." Quran 4:55 berates the Jew by saying, "Sufficient for the Jew is the Flaming Fire!"

Anti-Semitism is again on the rise in Europe with many occurrences coming from the rising Muslim communities. The individual heart-wrenching stories of hatred, persecution, physical harm, vandalism, and fear demonstrate why over half the Jewish population in the world has chosen to move to Israel.

- Eighty-five percent of European Jews are afraid to reveal their Jewishness.
- England experienced record-breaking anti-Jewish incidents in 2016, which were an increase of 36 percent over the previous year (Community Security Trust).
- Germany recorded a 200 percent increase in hate crimes against Jews in 2015 (Germany's Ministry of Justice).

- Anti-Semitic acts in France were seven times higher this last decade than in the previous decade.
- Jews represent less than 1 percent of the population in France but experience 51 percent of racist attacks (French Interior Ministry).
- In Greece, 69 percent of adults hold anti-Semitic views.
- In the Swedish town of Malmo, Shneur Kesselman is the only rabbi for the 1,000 Jewish residents. In his ten years in the city, he has been attacked 150 times.
- Even in the United States, with religious tolerance and freedom of religion, anti-Jewish incidents are on the rise. The United States houses the second largest Jewish population in the world.
- In the first two months of 2017, ninety threats were documented against Jewish Community Centers and schools in twenty-seven states.
- The Anti-Defamation League reported an 86 percent increase in attacks on Jews or Jewish institutions in the first four months of 2017. The 2016 statistics had shown an increase of 34 percent.
- Almost 75 percent of Jewish college students in the United States have been exposed to some sort of anti-Semitic comments.

These statistics clearly point to a world that has never been able to accept the Jewish people as equal, but, instead, has continually persecuted those individuals who God calls His chosen people. Based on Jesus' words in Matthew 24, what we have seen in history and in the modern era is a pittance compared with the persecution in the last days.

If Jesus was also speaking about Christian martyrdom in Matthew 24, the world has seen millions killed for the name of Christ over the centuries. Christian martyrdom started at the hands of the Jews who did not accept what they deemed to be a new sect of Judaism. It didn't take long before Roman Emperor Nero blamed the Christians for burning down Rome in AD 64 that started the Roman persecution. Oppression continued for nearly two hundred years until Emperor Constantine legalized the Christian religion, which later became the state church of the Roman Empire.

In his book entitled *New Foxe's Book of Martyrs,* John Foxe shares the stories of hundreds of Christian martyrs from the time of the apostles up through 1997. It helps the reader understand the periods, players, and rationale for persecution throughout the centuries. The author states that in the 20th century alone, more Christians were killed for their faith than in all previous centuries combined.

A 2017 report by the Center for Studies on New Religions (GESNVR) determined that 90,000 Christians were killed for their beliefs worldwide in 2016. This amounts to one death every six minutes. One-third of the Christians killed were executed at the hands of Islamic extremists, with the others killed by state or non-state militants like North Korea and Boko Haram. The study also found that as many as 600 million Christians around the world were prevented from practicing their faith in 2016.

The Christian population in Iraq has plummeted from 1.5 million in 2003 to 275,000 in 2016 and could be extinct within a few years. Syrian Christians made up 30 percent of the population in the 1920s but only 10 percent in 2016. The world watched while ISIL beheaded twenty-one Coptic Christians in Egypt in 2015. ISIL burned down a church at Christmastime in 2015, two churches on Palm Sunday in 2016, and attacked many others. Amnesty International reported numerous Coptic Christian's homes have been set on fire with looting of property and personal attacks to their owners.

Since there is "nothing new under the sun," it is no wonder that Jews and Christians are being attacked worldwide in record numbers, in the name of Jesus. The Jews are being persecuted for "killing" Jesus while the Christians are martyred for following Him. But, the situation is going to get much worse—soon.

Revelation 13 lays out a dreadful scenario in which everyone in the world will be forced to worship the world leader known as the Antichrist. The religious leader supporting the Antichrist will "make the earth and those who dwell in it to worship the first beast (Antichrist)" (Revelation 13:12). He will make an image of the Antichrist and require everyone to worship it or be killed. In addition, he will make it compulsory for everyone to have the mark of the beast in order to buy or sell. However, God declares a terrible judgment on those who follow the beast:

> If anyone worships the beast and his image, and receives a mark on his forehead or on his hand, he also will drink of the wine of the wrath of God, which is mixed in full strength in the cup of His anger; and he will be tormented with fire and brimstone in the presence of the holy angels and in the presence of the Lamb. (Revelation 14:9b, 10)

What a horrible predicament to find oneself in! Do you follow Christ and die or deny Christ and live? Many people have to make that decision today but everyone will have to make it during this Tribulation period. And, based on the current increase in persecution/martyrdom and the fulfillment of other prophecies, that time is coming sooner rather than later.

By the way, it's a no-brainer for me to make that decision. I would rather suffer for my Lord and Savior Jesus Christ on this earth than to ever deny Him. I would rather encounter the wrath of ungodly men than the wrath of God. I would rather endure momentary light affliction which is producing for me an eternal weight of glory far beyond all comparison (2 Corinthians 4:17) than experience what might be a few more months of life. How about you? If you were to choose today, would you choose Jesus for eternity or your life temporarily? That is the most important decision you will ever have to make. Where will you spend eternity?

Prophecy 29

APOSTASY

At that time many will fall away and will
betray one another and hate one another.
(Matthew 24:10)

" Help, I have fallen, and I can't get up!" That phrase can
be heard on an advertisement geared toward elderly
people. In this postmodern era, it can also be applied to those
who call themselves "believers" but who have fallen away and
are not living for Jesus Christ.

To properly interpret the Bible, it's important to revert back
to the original languages of the Bible. Our English words do
not always have the same meanings as the Hebrew and Greek
words. In the passage above, the phrase *fall away* means to
deceive someone into ungodly conduct resulting in mischief.
Based on the Revelation 13 information discussed at the end
of Prophecy 28, one can see how that can happen.

Revelation 13 describes the Antichrist and his religious
leader who will manipulate the world into worshipping the
Antichrist and his image and taking a mark with his name. That
scenario could certainly be the catalyst for deceiving people
into ungodly conduct, causing them to fall away from the truth.
However, someone doesn't easily become an apostate unless
he has already begun a downward spiral.

In the introduction, I listed many statistics to prove how people who have been raised in a Christian background have been steadily turning away from Jesus Christ for decades. In review, slightly more than 1 percent of the population of Great Britain attends church each week. While 64 percent of French citizens are Catholic, only 4.5 percent practice their faith. Only 9 percent of adult Americans hold to a very basic biblical worldview. Less than 1 percent of people born between 1982 and 2002 hold a biblical worldview. Twenty-two percent of young American adults ages 18–29 now consider themselves nonreligious.

Humans are different from other created things in that God made us in His image (Genesis 1:26). That doesn't mean we look like God physically. Instead, we uniquely possess a spirit like Him because "God is spirit and those who worship Him must worship in spirit and truth" (John 4:24). Therefore, God has given us a spirit, so we can relate to Him and have a relationship with Him. But, if we don't guide our spirit in the right direction, we will find spiritual food elsewhere.

The New Age movement surfaced in the 1970s, offering new spiritual enlightenment. Channeling with angels or deceased humans provided a guide to life and purpose for New Agers. Humanism took hold a few centuries before by putting mankind at the center of their universe rather than God. Evolution took God out of creation in the mid-1800s by "scientifically" stating that humans evolved from animals. The Big Bang Theory later identified an originating single point of creation, not from God but from some cosmic expansion. Over time, the world has thrown these and so many other theories and spiritual beliefs into a pot, allowing people to pick and choose what they want to believe, what makes sense to them, and what fits into their lifestyle. Some people start calling evil good and good evil (Isaiah 5:20).

Without a solid spiritual foundation of truth on which to stand, everyone is open to manipulation and misinformation. The Bible was the main school textbook in this country until it was taken out of the public schools in 1963. Subsequently, public school curriculum has changed to remove Christian principles and wording, to rewrite our Christian heritage, to include information about other religious cultures, to inform children on usage of sinful practices (sexual paraphernalia), to encourage and support deviant behavior, and to teach worldly values but not biblical ones. Add Hollywood and other forms of media to the mix, and that fortifies the secular, self-centered, anti-God, and lustful influences necessary to turn an entire culture away from God in a matter of just a few generations.

Christians expect to learn the truth in church and to hear it from their pastors. Yet, according to a Barna Group survey, conducted in 2003, only 51 percent of American Protestant pastors hold a biblical worldview. George Barna defines a "biblical worldview" as belief in absolute moral truth as defined by Scripture, as well as acceptance of six core biblical beliefs: the accuracy of biblical teaching, the sinless nature of Jesus, the literal existence of Satan, the omnipotence and omniscience of God, salvation by grace alone, and the personal responsibility to evangelize.

Of the pastors surveyed, Southern Baptists held the highest biblical worldview at 71 percent, while United Methodists finished at the bottom with just 27 percent. Other Baptist churches ranked at 57 percent, nondenominational Protestant churches at 51 percent, charismatic or Pentecostal churches at 44 percent, and leading mainline denominations at just 28 percent.

A major Christian theological belief is that Jesus Christ was born of a virgin as explained in the gospel of Luke, chapter 1. Yet the majority of pastors in the United States do not agree with this biblical principle. *PrayerNet Monthly Newsletter* published a 1998 poll that questioned 7,441 Protestant clergy in the United States, regarding their view of the virgin birth. The results show the percentage of denominational pastors who did not believe in the virgin birth of Jesus Christ:

American Lutherans—19 percent

American Baptists—34 percent
Episcopalians—44 percent
Presbyterians—49 percent
Methodists—60 percent

A Barna Group survey conducted in 2016 showed that 57 percent of adult pastors and 64 percent of youth pastors have struggled with pornography at some time in their lives. In a survey conducted in 2006 and 2007 by R. J. Krejcir PhD with the Francis A. Schaeffer Institute of Church Leadership Development, his findings mirrored those of Focus on the Family to show that 89 percent of pastors considered leaving the ministry, 77 percent of pastors don't have a good marriage, 72 percent only read the Bible when preparing their sermon, 71 percent are burned out, 38 percent are divorced, and 30 percent have had a sexual affair with a parishioner.

It appears from those statistics that a high percentage of our pastoral leaders are struggling as spiritual leaders and/or straying from biblical truths. With some spiritual leaders not serving as biblical role models, it's no wonder the church members are falling away from the truth.

Look at what happened in Israel at the time of the judges. In just three generations, Israel turned from a God-fearing country to a godless nation. Judges 2 lays out the scenario by explaining:

> The people served the Lord all the days of Joshua, and all the days of the elders who survived Joshua, who had seen all the great work of the Lord which He had done for Israel. Then Joshua the son of Nun, the servant of the Lord, died at the age of one hundred and ten... All that generation also were gathered to their fathers; and there arose another generation after them who did not know the Lord, nor yet the work which He had done for Israel. (Judges 2:7, 8, 10)

By the end of the period of judges, the country had spiraled out of control for 350 years so that "everyone did what was right in his own eyes" (Judges 21:25b). When men turn away from God, they stop following His teachings. You may recall that Jesus summarized all the commandments into two directives stated in Matthew 22:37–39, "And He said to him, 'You shall love the Lord your God with all your heart, and with all your soul, and with all your mind.' This is the great and foremost commandment. The second is like it, 'You shall love your neighbor as yourself.'" Love is the catalyst for living out one's relationship with God. Without God, love wanes. The opposite of love is hate.

Jesus prophesied that in the last days people will betray one another and hate one another. Hatred takes many forms such as jealousy, anger, murder, slander, bullying, and deception. The reasoning in this godless era seems to be that if you don't agree with someone, you are justified to destroy their beliefs or character. For example, Christians who believe in traditional marriage between one man and one woman are called homophobes. People who share facts about radical Islam are labeled Islamophobes. Those who believe in secure borders are being tagged as racists. Civility has been replaced with divisiveness; turning the other cheek has been ignored in order to seek revenge; responsibility has been substituted with blame. Love has been relegated to a feeling that comes and goes rather than a permanent outgrowth of our relationship with Jesus Christ.

Do you have a firm foundation in Jesus Christ? Are Jesus and His word the foundation by which you see the world and make your decisions? If not, you are open to being manipulated by others into doing what seems right in your own eyes. "There is a way which seems right to a man, but its end is the way of death" (Proverbs 14:12).

Prophecy 30

LAWLESSNESS

And because lawlessness is increased, most people's love will grow cold. (Matthew 24:12)

Hollywood painted a picture of a lawless Wild West in the mid-1800s where gun-slinging bandits ruled the land, robbed stagecoaches, and terrorized new settlements. Yet, the Western frontier was a far more civilized, peaceful, and safer place with less crime and homicides per capita than American society is today. Broadening worldwide, rebellion, uncivilized behavior, a world of terror, dictators, and poverty have become rampant in lawless societies.

Simply stated, lawlessness is transgression of the law or a lack of civil order. When people take matters into their own hands, they focus on their goals rather than looking out for the good of others. The world is in a more chaotic state than ever before as people disregard the civil and spiritual order that God created.

Over the past twenty years, the United States has designated sixty organizations as foreign terrorist organizations (FTO) and four countries designated as state sponsors of terror. These states and organizations have been responsible for the deaths of millions of people in the name of patriotism, religion, or power. While they may adhere to their own individual rules, they do not follow the laws of a civilized society.

Most of the terrorist organizations follow radical Islamic rules and practices. They see non-Muslims as infidels who must be converted to their form of Islam and pay a *jizya* tax as a fee for protection or be killed. Between 2001 and 2014, there were 14,586 deadly Muslim terror attacks. Islamic terrorists use many verses from the Quran to justify their actions including Quran 9:5, which states, "slay the idolaters (all non-Muslims) wherever ye find them, and take them (captive), and besiege them, and prepare for them each ambush [*sic*]. But if they repent and establish worship and pay the poor-due, then leave their way free." Islamic terrorists also terrorize and murder fellow Muslims who do not hold to their specific radical beliefs.

Citizens in the United States have the right to peacefully demonstrate to make their views known. However, violent rioting and lawlessness have become prevalent in the past several years as people have taken matters into their own hands. The Universal Declaration of Human Rights declares a defendant innocent until proven guilty in a court of law. Yet those who do not agree with police action have taken to the streets in organized protests in cities like Ferguson, San Diego, Charleston, Tulsa, and Milwaukee, resulting in acts of violence, looting, and arrests.

Politically motivated individuals and groups have hired agitators to cause discord and to delegitimize their opponents. "He is not my president" protestors took to the streets for months in angry demonstrations over the 2016 presidential election results. Students on some college campuses have rioted in an effort to squelch the free speech and views of conservative speakers. Organized protestors have disrupted political town hall meetings. Free speech rallies have been cancelled due to obnoxious and unruly protestors.

Look at the current political situation in the United States that has resulted in a divided country. Democrats did not like the outcome of the 2016 presidential election, so most refuse to work with Republicans in Congress. Republican presidential candidates who said they would support the Republican nominee changed their tune when Donald Trump became the nominee. Republicans in Congress who do not like the president's methods have stonewalled his agenda, fighting him at every turn. Congress spends more time bashing those on the opposite side than producing legislation. The FBI and the Justice Department are investigating many alleged illegal actions and activities by political leaders of both parties. Is this political rivalry new? No! But, the public display of antagonism and the uncivil behavior is beyond that expected of a civil society.

The news media used to respect a code of conduct that required impartiality in reporting the news. They investigated stories and reported the truth. Now many journalists simply recite their biased propaganda, which helps to incite their followers to negative words and actions. They follow a double standard in unfairly applying different methods for different people based on their personal agendas. They editorialize with sound bites that agree with their views instead of investigative techniques to uncover the facts.

Consider some statistics that show an increase in lawless activity around the world:

- There has been a 560 percent increase in the number of violent crimes in the United States since 1960.
- The murder rate in the United States experienced its largest increase in forty-five years in 2015, with an 11 percent increase over 2014, which amounted to 4.9 deaths per 100,000 people.
- The United Nations Office on Drugs and Crime reported a global average intentional homicide rate of 6.2 deaths per 100,000 population for 2012.
- Chicago violence in 2016 surged 72 percent in murders and 88 percent in shootings over the previous year.
- In 2013, an estimated 24.6 million Americans aged twelve or older, representing 9.4 percent of the

population, had used an illicit drug in the past month. This number is up from 8.3 percent in 2002.

One out of every six American women has been the victim of an attempted or completed rape in her lifetime (14.8 percent completed, 2.8 percent attempted). The acts of lawlessness are outward signs of an inward problem. The world is spinning out of control because we have turned away from God. Consider how God describes people's hearts and actions in these last days before His return:

> But realize this, that in the last days difficult times will come. For men will be lovers of self, lovers of money, boastful, arrogant, revilers, disobedient to parents, ungrateful, unholy, unloving, irreconcilable, malicious gossips, without self-control, brutal, haters of good, treacherous, reckless, conceited, lovers of pleasure rather than lovers of God, holding to a form of godliness, although they have denied its power; avoid such men as these. (2 Timothy 3:1–5)

That certainly sounds a lot like the world today.

God explains the consequences of lawlessness in 1 Corinthians 6:9–10. "Or do you not know that the unrighteous will not inherit the kingdom of God? Do not be deceived; neither fornicators, nor idolaters, nor adulterers, nor effeminate, nor homosexuals, nor thieves, nor the covetous, nor drunkards, nor revilers, nor swindlers, will inherit the kingdom of God." On the other hand, God clarifies that we are to follow the law:

> But we know that the Law is good, if one uses it lawfully, realizing the fact that law is not made for a righteous person, but for those who are lawless and rebellious, for the ungodly and

sinners, for the unholy and profane, for those
who kill their fathers or mothers, for murderers
and immoral men and homosexuals and kidnap-
pers and liars and perjurers, and whatever else
is contrary to sound teaching, according to the
glorious gospel of the blessed God, with which
I have been entrusted. (1 Timothy 1:8–11)

Jesus predicted a downward spiral in society before His
return. He first explained in Matthew 24 what the condition
of the world would look like (wars, rumors of wars, famines,
earthquakes, pestilence). Then He zeroed in on personal issues
and attitudes (tribulation, martyrdom, hated by all nations,
apostasy, hatred, and lawlessness). The world is looking just
as Jesus said it would. But those situations will be magnified
significantly when people find themselves groping through the
Tribulation.

Prophecy 31

GOSPEL PREACHED TO WHOLE WORLD

This gospel of the kingdom shall be preached in
the whole world as a testimony to all the nations,
and then the end will come. (Matthew 24:14)

J esus called His followers to share the good news of the gospel
of Jesus Christ throughout the world (Matthew 28:19–20).
They began spreading the gospel message first in Jerusalem,
then Judea and Samaria, and eventually to the remotest part
of the earth (Acts 1:8). The apostles traveled primarily by foot
and ship in their valiant effort to reach the known world with
the good news of salvation through Jesus Christ. While those
means of transportation were highly effective, there were areas
in the world unavailable to this outreach. That has all changed
in this age of mass communication.

The gospel was primarily shared by word of mouth until
the gospels and epistles were written decades after Jesus' death
and eventually codified as the New Testament at the Council of
Carthage in AD 397. It was not until the invention of the printing
press that the Bible became available to the general public. The
first book published was the Latin Vulgate Gutenberg Bible in
1454. The first English translation of the Bible was completed
in 1611 under the direction of King James of England. Since

then, the Bible is the most purchased and read book of all times, with 3.9 billion copies sold in the past fifty years.

At least one book of the Bible has been translated into 2,932 languages of the more than 6,900 known living languages. The entire New Testament is available in 1,333 languages with the complete Bible translated into 553 languages. More than 2,300 languages across 131 countries currently have active translation and linguistic development work in progress (Wycliffe Global Alliance 2015). This means 92 percent of the world has access to some form of the Bible. Does that mean that the other 8 percent of the world population has never heard the gospel? No. God has opened the door through missionaries, satellite TV, Internet, short wave radio and other means of communication, so the whole world will be able to hear His message.

In our travels to Israel, we are always amazed to see Bedouins living in goat tents as their ancestors did thousands of years ago, except they now have cars, satellite dishes, and cell phones to connect them with the rest of the world. While only 20 percent of the world has access to TV, nearly 50 percent of the world population now uses the Internet with access to unlimited Bible broadcasts (including ours). Shortwave radio frequency energy is capable of reaching any location on the Earth with the proper equipment. SAT-7, the first Arabic language Christian satellite channel to broadcast into the Middle East, has a viewer reach of 230 million people in the Middle East and North Africa. Missionary work in Spain sends TV gospel programs to Morocco with many people there coming to faith in Christ. Dr. Hormoz Shariat, called "The Billy Graham of Iran," broadcasts 24/7 in Farsi to millions of TV viewers in Iran.

For those people groups who have not been reached with the gospel, that's where God steps in to show Himself to the world. Tom Doyle, in his book *Killing Christians: Living the Faith Where It's Not Safe to Believe,* documents several stories of how Jesus has appeared to people miraculously. Joel Rosenberg's book, *Inside the Revolution,* shares amazing stories of how people have come to Jesus through dreams, visions, and appearances. And, let's not forget that God reveals Himself through nature also. Romans 1:20 explains, "For since the creation of the world His invisible attributes, His eternal power and divine nature, have been clearly seen, being understood through what has been made, so that they are without excuse." With all these opportunities, it is no wonder that some people claim the gospel message has already reached 99 percent of the people in the world. No other generation has seen this percentage of the world exposed to the good news of Christ's salvation for a lost world. This prophetic fulfillment once again proves that the time for Christ's return is at hand.

Jesus said the end would come *after* the gospel has been preached to the whole world. It has already reached up to 99 percent of the world. Those people who have not yet heard the gospel message will have the opportunity to do so through miraculous means before Jesus returns. Revelation 14:6–7 declares:

> And I saw another angel flying in midheaven, having an eternal gospel to preach to those who live on the earth, and to every nation and tribe and tongue and people; and he said with a loud voice, "Fear God, and give Him glory, because the hour of His judgment has come; worship Him who made the heaven and the earth and sea and springs of waters."

God wants His gospel message of love and redemption shared and received by everyone in the world. "The Lord is not slow about His promise, as some count slowness, but is patient toward you, not wishing for any to perish but for all to come to repentance" (2 Peter 3:9). He will continue to use every means and opportunity to spread the good news of salvation through Jesus Christ until His return.

Prophecy 32

ONE-WORLD GOVERNMENT

Then there will be a fourth kingdom as strong as iron; inasmuch as iron crushes and shatters all things, so, like iron that breaks in pieces, it will crush and break all these in pieces. In that you saw the feet and toes, partly of potter's clay and partly of iron, it will be a divided kingdom; but it will have in it the toughness of iron, inasmuch as you saw the iron mixed with common clay. As the toes of the feet were partly of iron and partly of pottery, so some of the kingdom will be strong and part of it will be brittle. And in that you saw the iron mixed with common clay, they will combine with one another in the seed of men; but they will not adhere to one another, even as iron does not combine with pottery. In the days of those kings the God of heaven will set up a kingdom which will never be destroyed, and that kingdom will not be left for another people; it will crush and put an end to all these kingdoms, but it will itself endure forever. Inasmuch as you saw that a stone was cut out of the mountain without hands and that it crushed the iron, the bronze, the clay, the silver and the gold, the great God has made known to the king what will take place in the future; so the dream is true and its interpretation is trustworthy. (Daniel 2:40–44)

The prophet Daniel interpreted a dream for King Nebuchadnezzar of Babylon over 2600 years ago that specified world kingdoms that would control Israel throughout history. In the time of the final kingdom, Jesus Christ will return to establish and reign in His much-awaited kingdom on earth. For the first time since that prophecy was given, the world is in a position to see the development of that final one-world power.

The prophecy in Daniel 2 describes a statue with a head of gold, a breast of silver, a belly and thighs of bronze, legs of iron with feet partly of iron and partly of clay. Daniel explained to the king of Babylon that he, Nebuchadnezzar, was the head of gold. After him would arise three other kingdoms, which history has proven to be the Medo-Persian Empire, the Greek Empire, and the Roman Empire. Out of the fourth kingdom would arise a final divided kingdom that will be the last world kingdom before Christ returns to destroy it.

> A stone was cut out without hands (kingdom of Jesus Christ) and it struck the statue on its feet of iron and clay and crushed them. Then the iron, the clay, the bronze, the silver and the gold were crushed all at the same time and became like chaff from the summer threshing floors; and the wind carried them away so that not a trace of them was found. But the stone that struck the statue became a great mountain and filled the whole earth. (Daniel 2:34, 35)

Daniel had a similar vision fifty years later that also described these world kingdoms. In Daniel 7:7, the fourth beast was depicted as "dreadful and terrifying and extremely strong; and it had large iron teeth. It devoured and crushed and trampled down the remainder with its feet; and it was different from all the beasts that were before it, and it had ten horns." This kingdom was later interpreted in Daniel 7:23 as "The fourth beast will be a fourth kingdom on the earth, which will be different from all the other kingdoms and will devour the whole earth and tread it down and crush it." After this kingdom, the kingdom of the Messiah will be established (Daniel 7:26, 27). The passages above provide some clues that the final global kingdom will be an offshoot of the Roman Empire (Chart 10). This last kingdom includes the element of iron (strength), just as the fourth kingdom, so it must be associated with it. It will be a divided kingdom as history proves the Roman Empire was. It will be different from all the other kingdoms before it and will devour the whole earth and crush it. Finally, this kingdom will consist of ten horns which Revelation 17:12–13 describes as ten kings having ten kingdoms with power and authority.

This final world empire will be strong enough to force all the world to come under its authority. How is it possible to develop a one-world government when the world is full of autonomous nations? The European Union is an example of how this can happen.

When six European countries formed the European Economic Community, also known as the Common Market, in Rome in 1957, many students of prophecy saw this to be the revived Roman Empire as prophesied in Daniel. As this entity grew in power and importance, it became the basis for the European Union (EU) that was established in 1993. By the year 2017, the EU had grown to twenty-eight member states. These sovereign countries have exchanged their autonomy for open borders and a cohesive unity within Europe. In so doing, they must adhere to the political, economic, and monetary jurisdiction of the EU.

As explained in Prophecy 22, the United Nations has laid the groundwork for a one-world government because virtually all the nations are part of that entity. The UN has taken the leadership role in bringing all nations together in many areas, including their sustainable development program (Chart 11). The goal of this program is to divide the world into ten different regions for the redistribution of resources. Could these regions be the ten kings or kingdoms of Revelation 17? Sustainable development has had many names since its inception in 1972, but its consistent plan has been to control global environment, economics, agriculture, education, and gender equality. The nations are already interdependent in trade, finance, health, culture, travel, security, military, and food, so joining together in a one-world government to manage all of these areas is not far off.

Presidents of the United States, along with other national leaders, have seen the need for and promoted a new world order since World War I. H. G. Wells brought the idea to public light through his book *New World Order* in 1939 when he proposed a collectivist one-world state. He argued, "Nationalist individualism... is the world's disease. The manifest necessity for some collective world control to eliminate warfare and the less generally admitted necessity for a collective control of the economic and biological life of mankind, are aspects of one and the same process."

In a speech delivered in June 1945, President Harry S. Truman endorsed a world government when he said, "It will be just as easy for nations to get along in a republic of the world as it is for us to get along in a republic of the United States." Former New York Governor Nelson Rockefeller claimed in his book *The Future of Federalism* that current events make a compellingly demand for a new world order. He stated:

> The nation-state is becoming less and less competent to perform its international political tasks.... These are some of the reasons pressing us to lead vigorously toward the true building of a new world order... [with] voluntary service... and our dedicated faith in the brotherhood of all mankind.... Sooner perhaps than we

may realize... there will evolve the bases for a federal structure of the free world.

During a September 11, 1990 speech to Congress entitled *Toward a New World Order,* President George H. W. Bush stated, "The crisis in the Persian Gulf offers a rare opportunity to move toward an historic period of cooperation. Out of these troubled times... a new world order can emerge in which the nations of the world, east and west, north and south, can prosper and live in harmony.... Today the new world is struggling to be born." In a speech delivered in 2009, former President Barrack Obama agreed that, "All nations must come together to build a stronger global regime." Former Vice-President Joe Biden expressed his support when he said, "The affirmative task before us is to create a New World Order."

David Rockefeller, a United States banker who died in early 2017, said, "We are on the verge of a global transformation. All we need is the right major crisis and the nations will accept the New World Order." Nelson Mandela, former President of South Africa, acknowledged, "This new world order that is in the making must focus on the creation of a world of democracy, peace, and prosperity for all." In his 2015 encyclical supporting Sustainable Development, Pope Francis I called for a new system of global government to tackle unprecedented worldwide threats.

World leaders have been preparing for a global government for decades. Consider organizations like the Bilderberg Group, the Trilateral Commission, the Royal Institute of International Affairs, the Knights Templar, the Illuminati, the Council on Foreign Relations, and the Club of Rome. The groups are made up of the most powerful people in the world who select many of the world's leaders and determine the direction for the world.

While it seems impossible that powerful countries like the United States and Russia will submit their citizens to a one-world government that will have authority over them, such action is on the horizon. The slippery slope toward globalism starts with the individual. He needs a community that provides roads, work, security, public service, and all other amenities. When the local community becomes overloaded with the burden of governance, it looks to the state for help. When the state needs assistance with education, infrastructure, disasters, and medical aid, they submit to the rules of the federal government. When the nation is ready to implode under all the pressure, it looks to the international community. As David Rockefeller said, it will just take one major catastrophe for the nations to unite as a global entity. Could that catastrophe be the rapture of the church when untold millions will disappear, leaving countries in chaos?

Prophecy 33

GLOBAL LEADER

The beast that you saw was, and is not, and is about to come up out of the abyss and go to destruction... Here is the mind which has wisdom. The seven heads are seven mountains on which the woman sits, and they are seven kings; five have fallen, one is, the other has not yet come; and when he comes, he must remain a little while. The beast which was and is not, is himself also an eighth and is one of the seven, and he goes to destruction. The ten horns which you saw are ten kings who have not yet received a kingdom, but they receive authority as kings with the beast for one hour. These have one purpose, and they give their power and authority to the beast. (Revelation 17:8–13)

The world has seen the rise and fall of countless emperors, dictators, and religious leaders who have wielded power over their domains. But never has a global leader controlled all seven continents from both a secular and a religious perspective. Such a position was never possible until modern times as global entities unite to form a one-world government that will need a captain. That leader has been referred to elsewhere in this book as the Antichrist. When he takes control, the whole world will soon be thrown into chaos.

The general term *antichrist* is mentioned four times in the books of 1 and 2 John. This antichrist is described as a liar, as one who opposes the Father and the Son, as one who denies that Jesus is the Christ, and as the deceiver who denies the deity of Christ in the flesh (1 John 2:18, 2:22, 4:3; 2 John 1:7). While this spirit of antichrist is identified in these verses, no one person is ever called the Antichrist in the Bible. Antichrist is a term many people have adopted to depict the evil world leader of the last days whom the Bible calls by many names.

This Antichrist will first come on the world scene as a peace-maker. Daniel 9:26 explains that the people who destroyed Jerusalem and the temple after Christ died (Roman Empire in AD 70) will later birth "the prince who is to come." When the time is ready for "the prince who is to come" to appear, "he will make a firm covenant with the many for one week, but in the middle of the week he will put a stop to sacrifice and grain offering; and on the wing of abominations will come one who makes desolate, even until a complete destruction, one that is decreed, is poured out on the one who makes desolate" (Daniel 9:27). This prophecy depicts him as a peacemaker with the authority and ability to coerce the Jews into a seven-year agreement. But, halfway through those seven years, the Antichrist will stop the Jewish sacrifices and institute the abomination of desolation by taking "his seat in the temple of God, displaying himself as being God" (2 Thessalonians 2:4).

A similar passage in Revelation 6:1–2 depicts the Antichrist entering the Tribulation period riding on a white horse, with a victor's crown and a bow as he goes forth claiming victory. The fact that the Antichrist is wearing a crown and has a bow but no arrows indicates he gained victory without going to battle. In this day and age, that's called diplomacy. And what could be a better diplomatic coup than bringing peace to Israel?

Once the Antichrist gains this victory, his world peace will be short lived. The next two horses of the Apocalypse in

Revelation 6 describe how the rider of the horses takes peace from the world causing severe famine. The rider of the fourth horse mentioned in Revelation 6 brings death to one-fourth of the earth through sword, famine, pestilence, and wild beasts. It is not surprising that a man like this is described in Daniel 7:7, 25 as the "fourth beast, dreadful and terrifying and extremely strong... [who] will speak out against the Most High and wear down the saints of the Highest One, and he will intend to make alterations in times and in law; and they will be given into his hand for a time, times, and half a time" (3 1/2 years). Later in Daniel 11:37–39 it says:

> He will show no regard for the gods of his fathers or for the desire of women, nor will he show regard for any other god; for he will magnify himself above them all. But instead he will honor a god of fortresses, a god whom his fathers did not know; he will honor him with gold, silver, costly stones and treasures. He will take action against the strongest of fortresses with the help of a foreign god; he will give great honor to those who acknowledge him and will cause them to rule over the many, and will parcel out land for a price.

As mentioned in Prophecy 28, this Antichrist is identified in Revelation 13 as the beast who receives his authority from Satan, will be worshipped by the people, and will force the world to take his mark in order to buy and sell. He will make war against the saints and "authority over every tribe and people and tongue and nation was given to him" (Revelation 13:8).

Revelation 17 describes the Antichrist as a scarlet beast, being ridden by Mystery Babylon (see Prophecy 34) and having seven heads and ten horns. The writer later explains in that chapter that the seven heads represent seven kings, which were actually past nations, with the Antichrist being an eighth and one of the seven. The ten horns are ten kings who will receive power and authority and give it to the beast. They will then attempt to wage war against Jesus Christ. While these descriptions seem a little strange to us, they paint a picture of a man who will have world power and authority and use that to fight against God. This will be Satan's one final attempt to destroy Jesus Christ. Fortunately, we know the rest of the story. Once again, Satan will lose. The Antichrist's reign will be short-lived, only seven years, and will be accompanied by wars and chaos. According to Daniel 9:27, the Antichrist will eventually come to complete destruction. Upon Christ's return, Jesus will judge this beast and throw him alive into the eternal hell that burns with brimstone (Revelation 19:20). Satan will be bound in the abyss for 1000 years (Revelation 20:1–3) but will be released one final time before joining the Antichrist in eternal hell.

There are many additional passages in Scripture that give us glimpses into the character and actions of this malicious man, the Antichrist. I think you get the picture. Remember, he will be empowered by Satan, so he will be a deceiver, who looks really good on the outside but is full of evil intent on the inside. He will say and do whatever is necessary to convince the world that he is their "savior," both politically and spiritually. And many in the world will buy it!

The time is ripe like never before for a global leader to rule over a one-world government. He may be on the rise to power today, though not yet known by the general populous as the future world leader. As stated previously, all it will take is one good, worldwide catastrophe to bring this prophecy to fruition. And with the way things are going in the world today, that could happen at any time.

Prophecy 34

ONE-WORLD RELIGION

Then one of the seven angels who had the seven
bowls came and spoke with me, saying, "Come
here, I will show you the judgment of the great
harlot who sits on many waters, with whom the
kings of the earth committed acts of immorality,
and those who dwell on the earth were made
drunk with the wine of her immorality." And he
carried me away in the Spirit into a wilderness;
and I saw a woman sitting on a scarlet beast, full
of blasphemous names, having seven heads and
ten horns. The woman was clothed in purple
and scarlet, and adorned with gold and precious
stones and pearls, having in her hand a gold cup
full of abominations and of the unclean things
of her immorality, and on her forehead a name
was written, a mystery, "BABYLON THE
GREAT, THE MOTHER OF HARLOTS AND
OF THE ABOMINATIONS OF THE EARTH."
And I saw the woman drunk with the blood of
the saints, and with the blood of the witnesses
of Jesus. When I saw her, I wondered greatly.
(Revelation 17:1–6)

My Jewish friends often joke that when you have five Jews in a discussion, they will have five different opinions. That's true with other people groups as well. So how is it possible to unite over 4000 religious groups in the world under one religious leader and philosophy when they all have different beliefs and traditions? I can't answer that, but I can tell you that, based on the Bible, it will happen.

The passage above introduces the great harlot described here as a woman. A harlot is a term used in the Old Testament as an analogy for false religions. Leviticus 20:5–6 shows the comparison: "I will cut off from among their people both him and all those who play the harlot after him, by playing the harlot after Molech. 'As for the person who turns to mediums and to spiritists, to play the harlot after them, I will also set My face against that person and will cut him off from among his people.'"

In the end times religious system, the harlot will dominate all the "peoples, and multitudes and nations and tongues," as explained in Revelation 17:1b, 15. That will be possible because of the joint acts of immorality with the "kings of the earth," forging an alliance that unites church and state. Clearly the whole earth will be seduced with the euphoria and power of her false pretenses and worship.

The harlot is seen in this passage as riding the beast, which is described exactly as the Antichrist in Revelation 13:1, proving the mutual religious and political relationship between the harlot and the Antichrist. It is interesting that outside an EU building in Brussels there is a statue depicting a woman riding a beast. This image is also displayed on a 2 Euro coin. Many believe this statue represents the mythological story of Europa and Zeus. Or, could it be that the EU sees itself as the revived Roman Empire, the final world power as outlined in the Bible?

This false religious system enjoys great wealth, as depicted in the harlot's clothing, perhaps from her compromising acts of godless indulgence and immorality. In other words, the harlot, just like the Antichrist, looks good enough on the outside to fool the people but her heart is full of abominations.

The name on the harlot's forehead associates her with Babylon, where the great apostasy first began at the Tower of Babel (Genesis 11:4). At Babel, the people decided to build a tower to reach the heavens and make a name for themselves. In attempting to build the tower of Babel, they disobeyed God's directive to scatter throughout the earth. They were putting themselves, their desires, and their fame before God. The history of the city of Babylon thereafter is associated with spells, sorcery, idol worship, and graven images (Isaiah 47:12, 13; Jeremiah 50:1, 2, 38). That is not surprising since Babylon's founder was Nimrod, which means "we shall rebel" (Genesis 10:8–10). Through him the ancient Mother-Son cult worship began.

Tradition says that Nimrod married his mother Semiramis. After his untimely death, his mother/wife commemorated him as a spirit being. She became the "Queen of Heaven" and Nimrod, being her son, became the "Divine Son of Heaven." Over time, Nimrod was considered a (false) Messiah, the son of Baal. Babylonians also worshipped their chief pagan god Marduk, also named Bel, as mentioned in Jeremiah 50:3. The Ishtar gate in ancient Babylon was named after their main goddess of love, fertility, and war.

The city of Babylon was considered the largest city in the world in the 7th century BC. During that time, the kingdom of Babylon gained ruthless control over most of the known world including Israel where they spilled the blood of the saints. Based on that history, Babylon has always been associated with apostate idolatry, evil, power, and murder. Since the harlot of Revelation 17 is called Babylon the Great, the Mother of Harlots, she is connected with those characteristics as previously described.

At the time of the final global government, the harlot will be directly involved with the Antichrist in the martyrdom of those who follow Jesus Christ since the harlot is described as "drunk with the blood of the saints, and with the blood of the witnesses of Jesus" (Revelation 17:6). The relationship between the false religious system and the Antichrist's political government in Revelation 17 dovetails exactly with the same systems described in Revelation 13.

A second beast is described in Revelation 13:11–15 as having "two horns like a lamb and he spoke as a dragon." This sounds like a person who will be considered a religious leader (as Jesus is the Lamb of God) but who will serve Satan. He is empowered with amazing ability to deceive people with signs and wonders. He will coerce those who dwell on the earth to worship the Antichrist both individually and through an image of the Antichrist, or they will be killed. Does that sound familiar? King Nebuchadnezzar of Babylon required all in his kingdom to bow down and worship a golden image of himself in the seventh century BC. Shadrach, Meshach, and Abednego were thrown into the fiery furnace for refusing that order (Daniel 3).

This second beast is called the "false prophet" in Revelation 19:20. He will force all the people to prove their worship to the Antichrist by receiving his mark on their right hand or forehead. However, everyone who does that will incur the wrath of God and be tormented with fire and brimstone (Revelation 14:9, 10).

Eventually, the Antichrist will declare himself to be God (2 Thessalonians 2:4), and he will have no further need to partner with the false religious system. He and the political leaders will hate the harlot, make war with her, and destroy her (Revelation 17:16). Ultimately, Christ will return, seize the beast and false prophet, and throw them alive into the eternal hell (Revelation 19:20).

Now, the question is, who and what is this false religious system? For centuries people thought it was the Roman Catholic Church since it has been the largest religion in the world (1.285 billion followers in 2017), is extremely wealthy, and is based in Rome, the city of seven hills (Revelation 17:9). However, Protestantism is following closely behind in adherents with

800 million followers in 2017. Or, maybe all the Christian denominations will form an alliance. This is actually already in the works.

The World Council of Churches (WCC) was established in 1948 as an international fellowship of churches seeking unity and a common witness of Christian service. While the Roman Catholic Church is not a member, the WCC includes 349 global and national Christian churches. The Roman Catholic Church has been reaching out to faith groups in other ways. They have signed a Joint Declaration on the Doctrine of Justification with the Lutheran World Federation in an attempt to bring the Catholics and Lutherans together. Pope Francis recently insinuated that most in the world serve the same God when he said, "Jesus Christ, Muhammad, Jehovah, Allah. These are all names employed to describe an entity that is distinctly the same across the world."

Another ecumenical movement to bring all faiths together worldwide began in 1893 with a conference called the Parliament of the World's Religions. Today there are over thirty international and national interfaith organizations working toward this end. The first Tri-Faith Initiative has formed in Omaha, Nebraska to bring Christians, Jews, and Muslims together in one complex which consists of a church, synagogue, mosque and community center to support and fellowship with one another. And a diverse group of global religious leaders, including Pope Francis and the Dalai Lama, met at The Hague in the Netherlands in June 2017 to appeal for religious fellowship and unity.

Could this final religious system unite the world under Islam instead of a form of Christianity since it will become the largest world religion by the mid-21st century? If the Antichrist is a Muslim, it is very possible he will require the world to submit to Allah and Islam. After all, the growth of Islam from the time of Muhammad has generally been accomplished through both an increasing birth rate and forced conversion.

Christianity has been the dominant world religion since it was declared the religion of the Roman Empire by Constantine the Great (AD 306–337). The religious world began to shift once Muhammad firmly established Islam through holy war. According to Mark Gabriel, a former Islamic Imam and professor at Al-Azhar University in Cairo, in his book *Jesus and Muhammad,* Muhammad won a major victory at the Battle of Badr in AD 624 that made him the strongest leader in Arabia. After that, Muhammad received new revelations instructing him and his followers to kill all infidels.

> Kill the Mushrikum (pagans) wherever you find them, and capture them and besiege them, and lie in wait for them in each and every ambush" (Surah 9:5). "Fight against those who (1) believe not in Allah, (2) nor in the Last Days, (3) nor forbid that which has been forbidden by Allah and His Messenger (Muhammad), (4) and those who acknowledge not the religion of truth (i.e. Islam) among the people of the Scriptures (Jews and Christian) until they pay the Jizyah (tax) with willing submission, and feel themselves subdued. (Surah 9:29)

Within 100 years after the death of Muhammad, Islam became a dominant force by "converting" people from the Middle East to northern Africa and west to Spain (Chart 12). Most Muslims today follow these religious principles to convert non-Muslims, just as Christians desire to convert non-Christians. Some Muslims proselytize peacefully while others do it through forced jihad (fighting against the enemies of Islam). Either way, Islam gained much power and land control in just one hundred years. It could happen again in modern times.

Consider that the top four religions worldwide—Christianity, Islam, Hinduism, and Buddhism—encompass 85 percent of the world population. The next dozen religions total 7 percent of the world population with the final 8 percent including all other religions. Most of the over 4000 religions are diametrically opposite in belief, worship, and lifestyle. Yet, a world religious leader will arise alongside the Antichrist who will show such signs and wonders so as to mislead, if possible, even the elect. The fact that the harlot of Babylon is referred to as a "mystery" means that we cannot completely understand who she is or what exactly she will do until the time comes. But, we do know she represents an apostate one-world religious system that will exercise religious control in the last days. Based on all the facts presented in this book, it looks like that time is coming sooner rather than later.

Prophecy 35

TECHNOLOGY

And it was given to him to give breath to the image of the beast, so that the image of the beast would even speak and cause as many as do not worship the image of the beast to be killed... and he provides that no one will be able to buy or to sell, except the one who has the mark, either the name of the beast or the number of his name. (Revelation 13:15, 17)

A statement is attributed to Charles H. Duell, commissioner of US Patent Office in 1899, who resigned because, in his opinion, "Everything that can be invented has been invented." He must not have understood the Bible, or he would have known that advanced technology would be needed to fulfill future Bible prophecy. Never before in all of human history could the prophecies mentioned in this chapter be ready to be fulfilled until modern technology became available.

Image of the Beast

The first time I visited Disneyland, I was mesmerized by a talking hologram in the Haunted House. That technology is so commonplace now that in 2014 Turkish President Recep Tayyip Erdogan addressed a meeting in Izmir, Turkey, as a hologram using special effects from Polyvision. Computer-generated imagery (CGI) is being used in Hollywood to seemingly bring deceased actors back to life. Photoshop can make people and things appear real when they are not. Motorola actually has a patent for a tattoo that will take commands from words in your throat that have not been vocalized. The tattoo will be emblazoned over your vocal cords to intercept subtle voice commands. These types of technology and more could be utilized during the Tribulation period to allow the image of the beast, as mentioned above, to speak. Nothing is as it seems anymore!

From the Hal 9000 computer in the movie *2001: A Space Odyssey* to Joshua in *War Games* to Google's "artificial moral reasoning" for driverless cars, the world has seen artificial intelligence (AI) advance at breakneck speed. Despite the use and promise that AI brings to a modern society, there are pitfalls in building machines that might become fully emotional and rational beings with a conscious and self-awareness, but soulless nonetheless. Perhaps an AI device made to resemble the Antichrist will be constructed to deceive the masses.

Mark of the Beast

Probably the best-known Bible prophecy dealing with advanced technology is the "mark of the beast" explained in Revelation 13:16–18. That mark will be required of all people on earth in order to buy or sell. It will be implanted on their right hand or forehead. This prophecy could not be fulfilled until the last fifty years. But even before that technology, certain other things had to be invented first.

In order to utilize modern technology, electricity would be necessary, which first became available in 1879. Next would come the invention of radio waves and the first radio broadcast in 1906. The first satellite was launched by Russia in 1957, providing for international communications. The Internet was discovered in the 1960s, and the World Wide Web was established in 1990. These technological advances, and more, would be necessary for the invention of the mark of the beast.

Most governments now require some type of national identification to identify their citizens. Passports were established in Europe during World War I and in the United States in 1918. They were followed in the United States with the issuance of a Social Security number for US citizens. Most passports and many credit cards now include a biometric chip for security purposes. The idea of using electronic means for security and personal identification has become the norm.

When we consider fingerprint technology (1891), DNA matching (1987), iris eye scanning recognition (1994), facial recognition advancements and national surveillance (Patriot Act of 2001), there are few places a person can hide today.

The idea of a universal system for buying and selling was first developed in 1974 with the Universal Product Code (UPC) barcode system. It was perfected and utilized in grocery stores and is now necessary for product inventory and sales purposes in most businesses. UPC barcodes, and so much more information, are currently available to be imprinted on human skin.

For at least a decade now, researchers have been perfecting an electronic tattoo, often called a BioStamp, which can be printed directly onto the skin. The sensors can be wired to monitor health conditions, much like a FitBit or an Apple watch do. The BioStamp is more sophisticated as it can monitor and send signals directly to your doctor. Just as smart phones can be used to open doors, turn on lights, and pay for purchases, these BioStamps are being programed to meet medical, governmental, and business demands. If this doesn't satisfy the mark of the beast creators, there are lots more identification options.

In 2004, PositiveID (formerly known as VeriChip) was developed with radio-frequency identification (RFID) to identify and track cattle, pets, and potentially even children. The device contains a unique identification number that can be linked to a database for identity, medical records, and other uses. About the size of a grain of rice, it is implanted under the skin and could be used with their other products like VeriMed, VeriGuard, VeriKid, and VeriPay. VeriChip needs a permanent power supply that could be obtained through Thermo Life, which operates off human body temperature. Or, it could be powered with a long-lasting lithium battery, gaining its strength through body heat. The forehead generates the most body heat along with the hand, which is where the mark of the beast will be implanted. In 2010, PositiveID/VeriChip was pulled from manufacture and marketing, perhaps due to FDA concerns over electrical burns, tissue reaction, and other health risks. Note that those who accept the mark of the beast will be smitten with loathsome and malignant sores (Revelation 16:2), perhaps as a result of this or a similar device that has not been properly tested.

There are so many more examples of modern-day conveniences that consumers are eager to use without considering the consequences. For example, universities such as Georgia Southern have deployed iris biometrics for entrance into its dining hall. Boston University's Marciano Commons uses fingerprint scanners in conjunction with contactless ID cards to access meals, payments, and verification. Palm scanners authorize account withdrawals for school meals in Pinellas County, Florida. Motorola has developed a microchip pill to be swallowed daily as a biological system to access cellphones, cars, doors, and other devices.

Ever since the September 11, 2001, terror attacks, US citizens have gradually given up their right to privacy with cell phones, street cameras, smart TVs, and computers in order to feel secure. This generation is also willing to give away their personal information through Facebook, Instagram, Twitter, and other social media options. It is not surprising that the world will be open to a chip or device that will be sold as another convenience.

Global Communication

In the middle of the Tribulation period, God's two witnesses, who have been prophesying and performing miracles for the previous forty-two months, will be killed by the Antichrist. Revelation 11:8, 9 explain what happens afterward:

> And their dead bodies will lie in the street of the great city which mystically is called Sodom and Egypt (Jerusalem), where also their Lord was crucified. Those from the peoples and tribes and tongues and nations will look at their dead bodies for three and a half days, and will not permit their dead bodies to be laid in a tomb.

The phrase "peoples and tribes and tongues and nations," or a similar variation, is used seven times in the book of Revelation to portray all the people on the earth. The passage above states that the whole world will be able to see these dead prophets. In order for that to happen, either everyone needs to be in Jerusalem, which is impossible, or they will see the bodies through TV, Internet, cell phones, or satellite. Every moment of every day the Western Wall Heritage Foundation has cameras running live on the Wailing Wall in Jerusalem. If the prophets lay in that location, the world can watch them 24/7.

Matthew 24:30 may paint a similar picture of a need for international viewing when Jesus returns. The passage reads, "And then the sign of the Son of Man will appear in the sky, and then all the tribes of the earth will mourn, and they will see the Son of Man coming on the clouds of the sky with power and great glory." While those who see Christ's return are not listed the same way as in Revelation, it is clear that all the world will see Jesus when He returns. It will undoubtedly be a supernatural phenomenon when the heavens open and Jesus descends riding on a white horse (Revelation 19:11). Or, perhaps those who have turned away from Jesus will have to watch it on CNN.

We live in a generation that can see just about anything happen in real time. That means these prophecies can be fulfilled at any time.

Nuclear Fallout

The world was not prepared for the carnage it saw when the "Little Boy" atomic bomb was dropped over Hiroshima, Japan on August 6, 1945 and the subsequent "Fat Boy" plutonium bomb fell over Nagasaki, Japan three days later. At Hiroshima, the only remains of people caught in the open were their shadows burned into stone. Nearly 300,000 people died instantly from the aftermath of radiation at both sites. This was the first and last time a weapon of mass destruction has been used in the world. As bad as those images are, the idea of a nuclear holocaust would be even greater. That description can be found in the Bible.

Zechariah 14 begins with the description of an end times war in Jerusalem. As the chapter progresses, verse 12 lays out a graphic description of the consequences that befall those who war against Jerusalem. It reads, "Now this will be the plague with which the Lord will strike all the peoples who have gone to war against Jerusalem; their flesh will rot while they stand on their feet, and their eyes will rot in their sockets, and their tongue will rot in their mouth."

According to the Campaign for Nuclear Disarmament, "The heart of a nuclear explosion reaches a temperature of several million degrees centigrade. Over a wide area the resulting heat flash literally vaporizes all human tissue." That sounds like people will virtually melt in a nuclear blast, just as described in Zechariah.

Luke 21:26 is a companion passage to Jesus' description of end times events from Matthew 24. In Luke's account he adds, "men fainting from fear and the expectation of the things which are coming upon the world; for the powers of the heavens will be shaken." While this could explain the plethora of heavenly occurrences mentioned in the Book of Revelation, it could also reflect the aftermath of a nuclear explosion. After all, the mushroom cloud over Hiroshima was reported as reaching 60,000 feet in the air.

Currently, nine countries have developed a nuclear weapons program, generally as a deterrent to invasion by others: United States, United Kingdom, France, Russia, China, Pakistan, India, North Korea, and Israel. Iran is working toward developing a nuclear program by the end of the Joint Comprehensive Plan of Action agreement in 2025. In order to protect themselves from a nuclear Iran, many Middle Eastern countries like Saudi Arabia, Egypt, Turkey, and others are looking to develop nuclear capabilities of their own. It only takes one rogue leader or nation to set off a nuclear weapon.

The book of Revelation details two major end times wars that will see the destruction of nearly half of the world's population within just a few years. During the first war, explained in the unveiling of the fourth horse of the Apocalypse in Revelation 6:7–8, one-fourth of the world will be killed. In the next war, outlined in Revelation 9:13–21, one-third of the world will be killed. When you consider that less than 3 percent of the world population died or was injured in each of the two world wars, there is no comparison to anything like this ever occurring in all of human history. It seems highly unlikely that those huge numbers could die in these two wars unless they are nuclear wars.

While these prophecies have not yet been realized, the technology now exists for them to occur at the proper time. Clearly, advanced technology has allowed for the fulfillment of prophecies that could never have been completed before these modern times.

Prophecy 36

INCREASED KNOWLEDGE

> Now at that time Michael, the great prince who
> stands guard over the sons of your people, will
> arise. And there will be a time of distress such
> as never occurred since there was a nation until
> that time... But, as for you, Daniel, conceal
> these words and seal up the book until the end of
> time; many will go back and forth, and knowl-
> edge will increase. (Daniel 12:1, 4)

In the 1960s, the large department store where my father worked housed a computer that filled a huge room. Now that information could be housed in a small fraction of the space. The last one hundred years have not only introduced the world to more efficient ways of communication but have perfected them to form an Information Age that no one could have anticipated.

Knowledge Increases

Since the early 1900s, the world has experienced a shift from the Industrial Revolution to the Information Age, which started with mechanical and analog electronic technology and progressed to the digital electronics of the 1980s. The original concept for a programmable computer was developed by

Charles Babbage in the mid-19th century. It wasn't until 1906 that his son, Henry, was able to give a successful demonstration of its usage.

Different companies experimented with analog, electromechanical, vacuum tube, and other types of computers until the integrated circuit was developed in 1952. Recognized companies like Toshiba and Hewlett Packard created their first computers in 1954 and 1956, respectively. The first person to coin the term "personal computer" was Ed Roberts who introduced the Altair 8800 in 1975. This was quickly followed by IBM's 5100 later that year. Apple weighed in with a better and lighter computer in 1976. Commodore, Compaq, Dell, and others quickly followed. With the introduction of personal computers came the advancement of the Internet.

The Internet was first invented in the mid-1960s for military purposes and expanded, so scientists could communicate. In 1971, email was invented. However, one of the most important inventions was that of the World Wide Web introduced in 1990 by Tim Berners-Lee at CERN (the European Organization for Nuclear Research). With browsers to surf the Internet, people can do almost anything from their computers. The International Telecommunication Union estimated that 3.2 billion people, nearly half the people in the world, were online in 2015. Virtually every piece of information available is at people's fingertips all the time! Through this advanced technology, it is no wonder that information has increased and has been made available to more people than ever before.

Buckminster Fuller, renowned 20th century inventor and visionary, created the "Knowledge Doubling Curve." He noted that until 1900 human knowledge doubled approximately every century. By the end of World War II, knowledge was doubling every twenty-five years. Today, things are not as simple because different types of knowledge have different rates of growth. For example, nanotechnology knowledge is doubling every two years and clinical knowledge every eighteen months. On average, human knowledge is doubling every thirteen months. According to IBM, the build-out of the "Internet of things" will lead to the doubling of knowledge every twelve hours (April 19, 2013 article by David Russell Schilling at www.industrytap.com).

The Daniel prophecy referenced above identifies the timing of the Tribulation period as the end times when this knowledge will increase. The distress that will occur like never before matches with Jesus' warning of the Tribulation period in Matthew 24:21. He said, "For then there will be a great tribulation, such as has not occurred since the beginning of the world until now, nor ever will." The evidence proves that this generation has and will continue to see knowledge expand at an astronomical rate, which means we are nearing the end of days as prophesied by Daniel.

The increase of knowledge in the last days may have another explanation for its fulfillment. The increase in knowledge could be an increased understanding of Bible prophecy and seeing signs of prophetic fulfillment. The late Elbert Peak (1920–2010) from Abilene, Texas, spoke at a conference in 1995 on the "Signs of the Times." He said, "Sixty years ago when I first started preaching, you had to scratch around like a chicken to find one sign of the Lord's soon return. But today there are so many signs I'm no longer looking for them. Instead, I'm listening for a sound—the sound of a trumpet" (*Bible Prophecy Insights* June 2009 edition 3).

Daniel was told to "conceal the words of the book" until the end of time when knowledge would increase. For centuries, it was difficult for Daniel's prophecies to be understood or to see their possible fulfillment without the advantage of history and current events. With current knowledge, students can determine the nations prophesied in Daniel 2, 7, and 8. History proves the kings and the battles depicted in Daniel 11. The "despicable person" and his actions described in Daniel 11 have been proven to be Antiochus Epiphanes IV, an example of the future Antichrist. The establishment of a final global government arising out of the old Roman Empire, as described throughout the Book of Daniel, can now be seen as a possibility. A peace agreement between the "prince who is to come" and the Jewish nation, as prophesied in Daniel 9:27, is a possibility now for the first time in 2500 years. One of the greatest biblical discoveries of the last century was that of the Dead Sea Scrolls found in caves in Qumran, Israel, in 1947. Copies of every book of the Old Testament, except the Book of Esther, were discovered, dating back to the 2nd century BC. The archeologists discovered eight manuscripts of Daniel that have been dated to near or before the time of Antiochus Epiphanes IV. That is significant as it proves an early dating to the 6th century BC for Daniel, thereby authenticating in these modern times that Daniel was written before the events prophesied in his book occurred.

Perhaps the knowledge that needed to increase is that of understanding Daniel's prophecies more than general knowledge. If so, this prophecy has been fulfilled. People are now able to read and understand the history and prophecies mentioned in the Book of Daniel.

People Will Go Back and Forth

Daniel 12:4 also states that in the end of time people will "go back and forth." Since this statement is made in the same context as the previous one about knowledge increasing, it should be looked at through the same lens. If the passage refers to general informational knowledge expanding, then people going back and worth would indicate people moving consistently from one place to another. This could be interpreted as meaning an increase in travel.

Before the 20th century, most people traveled less than thirty miles away from their homes in their lifetimes. Now, most of us put more than thirty miles on our cars each day! With transportation option such as trains, automobiles, modern ships, and airplanes, one can be anywhere in the world in a day. The first transcontinental airplane crossed over the English

Channel on July 25, 1909. The first commercial airplane flight occurred on January 1, 1914, from St. Petersburg, Florida to Tampa, Florida. The Soviet Union was the first country to put a human in space in 1961. Shortly thereafter, on July 20, 1969, the United Stated landed a man on the moon, opening the door for space exploration and for people to live in space stations.

If, however, the context of moving back and forth is associated with the increase in the knowledge of Bible prophecies, then people would be more diligently searching the Bible to better study and understand the prophecies of Daniel. That is certainly possible in the modern era through the printing of the Bible in original languages, reference books, commentaries, and Internet research.

The Hebrew words used in the phrase "go back and forth" indicate something that is happening within a person's mind as it moves back and forth contemplating a mystery or something they cannot figure out. The phrase could indicate stress that is caused by the mind being in constant turmoil over something that is burdening them. It could also indicate a widespread explosion of mental interest in and understanding of Bible prophecies. When I first began studying the Bible in the mid-1970s, I was curious as to these biblical prophecies and their impact on modern times. It was really difficult to find books on the subject except for a few written by authors like Hal Lindsey and Tim LaHaye. Now, the market is flooded with end times books dealing with every possible end times subject.

Whichever interpretations of the Daniel 12 passage that one adheres to, there is no question that the world has skyrocketed both in knowledge and in understanding of Bible prophecy, in travel, and in research of the Bible. These prophecies have been and are being fulfilled daily, like no other time in all of history.

Prophecy 37

WEALTH

Come now, you rich, weep and howl for your miseries which are coming upon you. Your riches have rotted and your garments have become moth-eaten. Your gold and your silver have rusted; and their rust will be a witness against you and will consume your flesh like fire. It is in the last days that you have stored up your treasure. Behold, the pay of the laborers who mowed your fields, and which has been withheld by you, cries out against you; and the outcry of those who did the harvesting has reached the ears of the Lord of Sabaoth. You have lived luxuriously on the earth and led a life of wanton pleasure; you have fattened your hearts in a day of slaughter. You have condemned and put to death the righteous man; he does not resist you. (James 5:1–5)

"It's the economy, stupid" is a slight deviation of a campaign slogan that James Carville hung in the Little Rock, Arkansas, headquarters of 1992 Presidential candidate Bill Clinton. That phrase has certainly taken hold in America, as it seems to be the number one issue on peoples' minds. Wealth has become so important in Western society that it is no longer simply a need but an idol.

Jesus said, "you always have the poor with you" (Mark 14:7). History and archeology prove that the rich we always have with us also. The difference in these last days is that more people have more wealth than ever before, and they are tucking it away for the future, just as James prophesied.

Why are people in the richest countries of the world so much wealthier today than one hundred years ago? C. I. Jones of Stanford University set out to answer that question by providing detailed statistics in an informative paper he wrote in 2016 called "The Facts of Economic Growth." Between the years 1 BC and AD 1820, living standards in the "West" doubled, from around $600 per person to around $1200 per person. Over the next hundred years, the gross domestic product (GDP) average per person rose by more than a factor of twenty, reaching $26,000. In recent years, GDP per person in the United States economy has grown at a remarkably steady average rate of around 2 percent per year. Starting at around $3,000 in 1870, per capita GDP rose to more than $50,000 by 2014, a nearly seventeen-fold increase. By 2016, the GDP per capita in the United States was $52,194. The financial successes in Western society continue to provide more opportunities and possessions than at any other time in history.

Retirement accounts continue to skyrocket also as people save more money for the future. The Investment Company Institute reports that as of March 31, 2017, Americans held $26.1 trillion in US retirement assets. CBS News reported on March 9, 2017, that United States household wealth in the final three months of 2016 was almost $93 trillion. Wealthy Americans continue to prosper, as 10 percent of them own 80 percent of the stock market. It has been said that even the poorest of those in the United States are richer than 95 percent of those in other parts of the world.

Based on a November 6, 2016 article by Kim Iskyan of Stansberry Churchouse Research, the total value of the world's stock markets has risen 133 percent since 2003 to a value of $69 trillion for the sixty major countries. In January 2018, value in the US stock market topped $30.6 trillion, a 23 percent increase over the previous year. China's market cap has grown an incredible 1479 percent since 2003, to be worth more than France, Germany, and Switzerland combined. While those statistics may seem boring to read, they establish an amazing pattern of financial and economic world growth over the past 150 years. All charts depicting wealth appear flatlined until the 1800s. They gradually rise until the 1900s at which time they have soared straight upward. Our world has never seen nor could ever have imagined the type of wealth it has achieved. Americans have and are storing up their wealth like never before as are individuals in other developed countries.

Being prosperous is one of the many blessings bestowed by God as He is the one who gives the abilities and opportunities to acquire wealth. The Bible is full of wealthy people. The Patriarchs of the Old Testament were well respected and prosperous in livestock, family, and land. King Solomon was the wealthiest of all kings because God blessed him for asking for wisdom rather than worldly possessions (1 Kings 3:9–13). Zacchaeus, the rich tax collector, was willing to give half of his possessions to the poor (Luke 19:8). Paul's traveling companion, Barnabas, sold his property and laid the money at the feet of the apostles (Acts 4:37, 37). Joanna and Susanna provided for the needs of the disciples out of their own resources (Luke 8:3). Joseph of Arimathea was a wealthy man and prominent member of the Council, who gave his tomb as Jesus' burial place (Matthew 27:57–60).

As in everything, finances are a responsibility that are to be used in a way that will honor God. That means attitude and actions must be focused on God's plan for the wealth rather than ours. The apostle Paul warns what will happen when responsibility morphs into an unhealthy desire for bigger, better, and more of what the world has to offer. In Timothy 6:9–10 Paul explains, "But those who want to get rich fall into temptation and a snare and many foolish and harmful desires which plunge men into ruin and destruction. For the love of money is a root of all sorts of evil, and some by longing for it have wandered away from the faith and pierced themselves with many griefs." Many people believe money will make them happy and solve all their problems. The reality is that only God can give us joy and solve the issues of life. Money will never satisfy. But that doesn't stop people from lusting after it. A friend once told me that she would be happy if she could have a diamond ring, a mink coat, and a fancy car. She died with several diamond rings, six mink coats, and a fancy car, but she still wasn't satisfied. "He who loves money will not be satisfied with money, nor he who loves abundance with its income. This too is vanity" (Ecclesiastes 5:10).

Jesus warned to "Beware, and be on your guard against every form of greed; for not even when one has an abundance does his life consist of his possessions" (Luke 12:15). He continued to explain the consequences of greed in a parable in Luke 12:16–21:

> The land of a rich man was very productive. And he began reasoning to himself, saying, 'What shall I do, since I have no place to store my crops?' Then he said, 'This is what I will do: I will tear down my barns and build larger ones, and there I will store all my grain and my goods. And I will say to my soul, "Soul, you have many goods laid up for many years to come; take your ease, eat, drink and be merry."' But God said to him, 'You fool! This very night your soul is required of you; and now who will own what you have prepared?' So is the man who stores up treasure for himself, and is not rich toward God.

Resources are to be used to provide for one's household (1 Timothy 5:8) and to take care of others. Paul explains that principle in Ephesians 4:28b, "Labor, performing with his own hands what is good, so that he will have something to share with one who has need. After all, we have brought nothing into the world, so we cannot take anything out of it either" (1 Timothy 6:7). The world's wealth and treasures are more abundant than ever. Opulence can be witnessed in bigger and better luxury homes, vehicles, yachts and expensive "toys." More money than ever is being put away for a rainy day just as God said would happen in the last days. If Jesus were to come today, would He see you enjoying a healthy portfolio and luxurious living accommodations or would He see a modest lifestyle on earth because you stored your riches in heaven?

> Do not store up for yourselves treasures on earth, where moth and rust destroy, and where thieves break in and steal. But store up for yourselves treasures in heaven, where neither moth nor rust destroys, and where thieves do not break in or steal; for where your treasure is, there your heart will be also. (Matthew 6:19–21)

Prophecy 38

TWO HUNDRED MILLION MAN ARMY

"Release the four angels who are bound at the great river Euphrates." And the four angels, who had been prepared for the hour and day and month and year, were released, so that they would kill a third of mankind. The number of the armies of the horsemen was two hundred million; I heard the number of them. (Revelation 9:14b-16)

The apostle John explains in this Revelation passage that he heard the number of an end times army to be 200 million. That is a huge army, nearly 1,000 times the size of the entire Roman army when John wrote this. As a matter of fact, the entire world population at the time of his writing didn't reached that number. Even though that size army seemed impossible, John wrote what he was told. Today, that size army is not only possible, but at least three options exist for it. It would seem logical that since the angels are bound at the Euphrates River, this army will come from east of the Euphrates River. There are three individual people groups today who could orchestrate that size army from that area: Chinese, East Indian, and the Muslims.

China is the most populous country in the world with 1.38 billion people of which 711 million are male. Males of potential fighting age of between fifteen and sixty-four equate to a possible 522 million man army. India comes in a close second with a population of 1.32 billion. Statistically, that would mean nearly 500 million men of fighting age live in India. Round those figures off with the fact that nearly 4.5 billion people live in the overall area of Asia as of August 2017, and you could have 1.5 billion men of fighting age from east of the Euphrates River coming together to wage war. In addition, about 60 percent of the 1.8 billion Muslim population are living in Asia. On an average, that would mean about 200 million Muslim men of fighting age would match the criteria set out in Revelation 9.

Hollywood has entertained us with the idea of robots and robot armies for decades. Dramatic and animated movies such as *The Terminator*, *Transformers*, *WALL-E*, *Iron Man* and loads more glorify the idea of androids, biomechanically engineered "people" and robots. With the race to build artificial intelligence (AI) robots for cars, homes, and businesses, anything is possible.

Top tech companies are investing billions of dollars to capture this massive new AI market. Generally this artificial intelligence has been used in areas like Apple's Siri, IBM's Watson, and Amazon's Alexa. But Google, Facebook, and Microsoft are devoting their research labs to AI robotics. Facebook has already revised one of its programs because their "bot to bot" conversation led to the development of its own language. The ability to create intelligent programs that can respond to every need, expand programs to take over human actions and reactions, and develop robots to replace certain job positions has opened the idea for robot or Android armies. The armed services are already using unmanned drones to gather intelligence and drop bombs. There are grave concerns for abuse, terroristic programming, and technological failures that should keep countries from actually employing an army of robots. But, like most other things, the world will see this as beneficial before someone misuses it with malevolent intent. While large-scale misuse is not yet on the horizon, the possibilities and technologies are.

Then, of course, there is the fear of alien invasion perpetrated by Hollywood ever since *The War of the Worlds* aired on October 30, 1938. The opening of Edwards Air Force Base Area 51 in Nevada in 1955 fueled rumors for UFO and conspiracy theorists. Is it possible the prophesied army could be made up of such creatures? After all, most people believe in them! In 2015, a market research company named YouGov found that 56 percent of Germans, 54 percent of Americans and 52 percent of British citizens believed that extraterrestrial intelligent life exists. The point here is that over 50 percent of the people in the world could accept the notion of an alien army.

On another note, the Scripture above as well as Revelation 16:12, explain that the 200 million man army will cross the Euphrates River. God could certainly dry up the river supernaturally. Or, it could happen through modern technology. The Atatürk Dam was completed in 1990 and is one of the five operational dams on the Euphrates River. By closing these dams, the Euphrates River could be completely dried up so that armies could march across it on dry ground.

The world population in 1800 was 904 million. By 1900, the world population reached about one billion. That means that only in the past several decades has it been possible for any part of the eastern world to muster an army of 200 million men who could cross the Euphrates River on dry ground. Certainly this war has not yet happened, but the circumstances for it to occur make it possible at any time.

Prophecy 39

BEHEADINGS

> Then I saw thrones, and they sat on them, and judgment was given to them. And I saw the souls of those who had been beheaded because of their testimony of Jesus and because of the word of God, and those who had not worshiped the beast or his image, and had not received the mark on their forehead and on their hand; and they came to life and reigned with Christ for a thousand years. (Revelation 20:4)

"Off with their heads!" Shakespeare first coined that phrase in his 1592 play *Henry VI*, probably due to infamous English beheadings such as Anne Boleyn, the second wife of Henry VIII, on trumped up charges of adultery. A few centuries later, the French used a more sophisticated guillotine to execute King Louis XVI and his wife, Marie-Antoinette, on counterrevolution charges. In this modern era, these methods of execution have mostly been abolished. While there are still a few countries that allow for beheading convicted criminals, beheading is best known as a modern method of terror by Islamic radical extremists who believe they are to annihilate the infidels. Could this be the type of Christian martyrdom outlined in Revelation 20?

Beheading is nothing new; it was an ancient practice mentioned several times in the Bible. David beheaded Goliath after striking him in the head with a stone (1 Samuel 17:51). The Philistines carried the head of slain King Saul throughout their land as good news that the king was dead (1 Samuel 31:8–10). King Saul's son, Ish-bosheth, was murdered by the sons of Rimmon the Beerothite who took his head to King David (2 Samuel 4). In the New Testament, as recorded in Mark 6:14–29, John the Baptist was beheaded by Herod Antipas.

The most practical method of execution throughout history has been beheading with the use of a sword or axe because those instruments were readily available. The Roman Empire would crucify enemies as it was more painful and humiliating, while they would execute their own citizens with a quick beheading. European countries continued the practice of beheading as late as 1938 in Germany until those nations abolished the death penalty. Countries like China and Japan have chosen hanging as their method of execution. Most countries in the world have discontinued the practice of beheading. Iran, Qatar, and Yemen still allow it but haven't used it in decades. Saudi Arabia is the only known country which uses beheading as their form of execution, generally averaging about 150 per year.

In the past, beheadings were used by authorities as a deterrent to criminals for illegal behavior. The tide has turned. Now, beheadings are a threat by criminals to authorities and the general public. The Islamic State of Iraq and the Levant (ISIL) has reestablished beheading as their preferred method of terror. Other terrorist groups like Boko Haram and Abu Sayyaf have followed suit. Hamas, the terrorist Palestinian organization that controls the Gaza Strip, has developed a project called Gazans United in Lessening Liberal Orientations toward Islam's Nefarious Enemies (GUILLOTINE). Schools in the Gaza Strip devote classroom time from kindergarten to college to teach methods of beheadings, and community centers train people to become proficient in the art of severing a human head with a blade.

There is a common denominator among these terrorist groups who murder by cutting off heads: they follow the extreme Islamic view of subjugating or killing everyone who is not a Muslim. Verses in the Quran provide their direction and methodology such as Quran 47:4, "Therefore, when ye meet the Unbelievers [in fight], strike off their heads." Quran 8:12 adds to that premise when it says, "I will instill terror into the hearts of the unbelievers: smite ye above their necks and smite all their finger-tips off."

While 25 percent of countries in the world still allow the death penalty for criminal offenses, all but one nation have done away with beheading as the procedure for that capital punishment. However, the Bible prophesies that beheading will be the method by which believers in Jesus Christ will be martyred during the Tribulation period. Will that occur because radical Muslims use this dominant form of torture or because the world will revert back to that simple method of execution? We don't know the answer but we do know that beheading has resurfaced at a time when dozens of other prophecies have been or can be fulfilled. Is that a coincidence?

Prophecy 40

EVOLUTION

Know this first of all, that in the last days mockers will come with their mocking, following after their own lusts, and saying, "Where is the promise of His coming? For ever since the fathers fell asleep, all continues just as it was from the beginning of creation." For when they maintain this, it escapes their notice that by the word of God the heavens existed long ago and the earth was formed out of water and by water, through which the world at that time was destroyed, being flooded with water. (2 Peter 3:3–6)

One day the zookeeper noticed that the monkey was reading two books—the Bible and Darwin's *On the Origin of Species*. In surprise he asked the ape, "Why are you reading both those books?" "Well," said the monkey, "I just wanted to know if I was my brother's keeper or my keeper's brother." While we might chuckle at that joke, we can't laugh at the fact that modern history has taken God out of creation. The reality is, we are gradually taking God out of everything. That is not surprising based on the sinful nature of man.

When God finished creating the world, He said, "It was very good" (Genesis 1:31). Shortly thereafter, however, Adam and Eve chose to disobey God and brought sin and death into the world (Genesis 3). As a result, "Death spread to all men, because all sinned" (Romans 5:12). It is this sin nature inhabiting every man (Romans 3:23) that gives us a desire to be master of our own universe and to make decisions contrary to God. In the process, mankind tends to ignore God and replace Him with someone or something else. In the case of creation, God has been replaced with the theory of evolution.

The concept of evolution can be dated as far back as the 6th century BC. The Greek philosopher Anaximander suggested that man had "evolved" from an earlier creature, such as a fish, which had "evolved" from the natural elements. A 9th-century Islamic scholar al-Jahiz theorized, "Environmental factors influence organisms to develop new characteristics to ensure survival, thus transforming them into new species." The great Swedish natural scientist Carl Linnaeus proposed a compromise between creation and evolution when he suggested in 1744 that God originally made just a few starting species. Over time, these species interbred, producing hybrids, resulting in a much broader range of species.

Modern evolution was first promoted by Charles Darwin in his book *On the Origin of Species* in 1859. He advocated a natural selection process by which organisms change over time as a result of changes in inherited physical or behavioral traits. Changes that allow an organism to better adapt to its environment will help it survive and have more offspring. Darwin's Theory of Evolution gained national consideration through the Scopes (monkey) trial in 1925. John T. Scopes was accused and convicted of violating Tennessee's law against teaching human evolution in any state-funded school. His conviction was overturned, which opened the door for states to rescind their laws restricting this type of teaching. Evolutionary instruction is currently advocated in every state in the United States, though many school systems also teach creationism.

The teaching of evolution varies worldwide. Communist countries strongly enforce its teaching while Muslim countries do not. The European Union's Parliamentary Assembly has taken a fairly strong stance on keeping evolution in the classroom. France requires that only scientific theories may be taught in the schools, while England allows for both evolution and creationism. Creationism has been believed and taught in schools until this modern era, but that has changed as God said it would.

People who have anxiously anticipated the imminent return of Jesus Christ have been mocked for their belief for two thousand years. But, it has only been in modern times that this mocking has been associated with an anti-creation viewpoint. In this era, people are ignoring that God is the Creator of the world. If we can take God out of creation, we can take God out of anything. If we have descended from apes or some plasma blob, we have no accountability to a Supreme Being. We can justify and do whatever we want. Society can and has developed its own plumb line for what is right and wrong. Men can and are doing what seems right in their own eyes (Judges 21:25). This last and final prophecy depicting Christ's soon return has been fulfilled over the past ninety years.

The world has arrived at the point in history when God is fulfilling His prophecies in preparation for the return of Jesus Christ. Only the generation living at the time of the first coming of Jesus Christ has seen as many fulfilled prophecies as this generation. That means you can expect that *Jesus is Coming…Soon*. It is time to "lift up your heads, because your redemption is drawing near" (Luke 21:28).

THE FINAL CHAPTER

"That's all Folks!" declares Porky Pig as he breaks through a drum head at the end of the Looney Tunes cartoons. One of these days, the world will experience all the prophecies mentioned in this book and more. At that time, "That's all Folks"—the end will come. But, it won't be Porky Pig poking through the screen. It will be Jesus Christ appearing in all His glory. When Jesus inspired the last book of the Bible, He declared "'I am coming quickly'" (Revelation 22:20). One generation in all of human history is guaranteed to see that event. Based on the proven prophecies in this book, it may well be our generation. If so, are you ready to face Jesus?

You may be like I was—you know about Jesus, you call yourself a Christian, you follow your religion, and you are a good person, but you do not have a relationship with Him. I was raised in a religious home, attended parochial schools, and followed my religion. However, it was not until I was twenty-four years old that I realized being a Christian means a personal relationship with Jesus Christ as Lord. It means accepting His free gift of eternal life by faith in His death on the cross for my sins and His resurrection.

Since the Bible is God's word to us, divinely inspired and accurate in everything, reading it is like sitting down and having a talk with Jesus. So let's see what God has to say in Romans 6:23 about how to obtain eternal life:

**For the wages of sin is death, but the free gift
of God is eternal life in Christ Jesus our Lord.**

As we discussed earlier, Adam and Eve brought sin into the world, which resulted in physical and spiritual death. These deaths spread to all men because all have sinned (Romans 3:23; 5:12–21). Sin separates man from God. It can be both willful rebellion against God or just simply ignoring Him. Sin means "to miss the mark" of God's commands, His word, and His truth. No matter what we try to earn, achieve or work toward, we are sinners. We miss God's mark; we are doomed to physical and eternal death away from God. Nothing can be done about physical death, but God has made a way so we do not need to die a spiritual death.

Picture people standing on one mountain and God standing on another mountain with a deep valley in between. That depicts how we are separated from God by the chasm of sin. There is no humanly possible way to reach God. *But*, God made a provision, a way to cross the divide of sin and spiritual death.

The word *but* in Romans 6:23 is a contrasting word, separating the first part of the verse from the second. It gives us a different option. Instead of being separated from God, it allows for a different eternal result.

This new option is a free gift from God. We can't purchase the gift. We can't manipulate a way to acquire it. We can't work for or earn the gift. We can't follow religious practices to obtain it. Only God provides the way for us to receive this free gift.

Jesus Christ is God, so He is the only bridge who can connect sinful man with our Holy God. Jesus declared, "I am the way, and the truth and the life; no one comes to the Father, but through Me" (John 14:6). Peter made this point clear in Acts 4:12, "And there is salvation in no one else (than Jesus); for there is no other name under heaven that has been given among men by which we must be saved."

The gift of God is eternal life through belief in Jesus Christ as our Lord. When our physical bodies die, our spirits will live on forever with God in heaven if we accept His gift. "For God so loved the world, that He gave His one and only Son, that whoever believes in Him shall not perish but have eternal life" (John 3:16).

God offers this free gift of eternal life through Jesus Christ to everyone, but it is our responsibility to accept it. So, now it's time to ask yourself, "Are you standing on man's sinful mountain or God's saved mountain?" There is no in-between, no gray areas with God. You can't have a foot on each mountain. You are either a sinner condemned to death or a sinner redeemed by the blood of the Lamb. You will either spend eternity in hell or eternity in heaven. Will you reach out and accept God's gift today?

Just as we reach out to accept a physical gift, we must reach out in faith to accept this spiritual gift. We do that through a personal act of humble and heartfelt prayer before God. First, we admit to God that we are sinners, separated from God. As such, we humbly repent of our waywardness from Him. We believe that Jesus Christ is God who died to take away the penalty for our sins and then rose from the dead to conquer spiritual death. We then commit our lives in faith to follow Jesus Christ as Lord. Do you believe these things and have you acknowledged them to God? If so, the Bible says you have eternal life right now just for believing! How amazing!

By faith in what Jesus did for us on the cross, we receive not only the free gift of eternal life but abundant life with Him here on earth. That does not mean we get everything we want and life becomes a rose garden. It means that we are now a new person in Christ: "If anyone is in Christ, he is a new creation, the old has gone, the new has come!" (2 Corinthians 5:17). The Bible explains it this way, "I have been crucified with Christ; and it is no longer I who live, but Christ lives in me; and the life which I now live in the flesh I live by faith in the Son of God, who loved me and gave Himself up for me" (Galatians 2:20).

This new life in Christ is an exciting one! Getting to know our God, seeing Him work in our lives and living for Him is better than anything you could ever have imagined. If you have committed your life in faith to Jesus Christ, we will see you in heaven! In the meantime, start looking at things on this earth through God's eyes, His plans and His grace. Begin your new life with Jesus by getting to know Him. Here are some helpful steps you can take:

1. Read the Bible.

   The Bible is inspired by God and 100 percent accurate in all teachings. It is the means by which we can get to know God and His directives for everyday living. Always begin with a prayer, asking God to speak to you through His word. Start reading the Gospel of John and then the rest of the New Testament. Gradually introduce the Old Testament, beginning with Genesis and alternating back and forth with the New Testament. As you read, ask yourself what the main truths are in each chapter. What do you learn about God the Father, Jesus Christ, and the Holy Spirit? Is there an example to follow, a sin to avoid, or a promise to claim?

2. Pray.

   Prayer is your communication with God. Talk with Him about the issues of life and problems. Confess your sins to Him. Ask for His guidance.

3. Meet with other Christians.

   God wants us to worship together, to encourage one another, to pray for each other, and to help one another in time of need (Hebrews 10:25). Look for a Bible-believing church where you can grow in your new faith. Join a Bible study to learn more of the Bible. You can also visit our website at www.livingwordministry.org to watch our Bible studies on YouTube and listen to our radio programs on current events in Bible prophecy.

4. Share your faith.

Tell others how you found God's forgiveness and His gift of eternal life in Jesus Christ.

May your joy be complete in Christ as you await His return. "Come, Lord Jesus! The grace of the Lord Jesus be with all. Amen" (Revelation 22:20b, 21).